HOW TO
ESCAPE
FROM

LLOYD EVANS

D1643387

HOW TO ESCAPE FROM JEHOVAH'S WITNESSES

BY
LLOYD EVANS

JLE Publishing
2018

Published by JLE Services Ltd. t/a JLE Publishing

www.reluctantapostate.co

April 2018 printing

Unless otherwise indicated, Scripture quotations are from the modern-language *New World Translation of the Holy Scriptures*, 2013 edition, published by Watchtower Bible and Tract Society of New York, Inc.

Certain references to Watchtower publications are provided in shortened form. For further information, see "Abbreviations of Publication Titles" in *Watch Tower Publications Index*.

Photo Credits: ■ Page 58: © Watch Tower Bible and Tract Society of Pennsylvania

Typeset in 12 pt/15 pt Alegreya Sans
DTP services provided by Toon Media Publishing

Cover design by Kyle Racki
Layout by Arthur Weber

How to Escape Jehovah's Witnesses

ISBN: 978-0-9956691-5-4 (paperback);
978-0-9956691-6-1 (Kindle)

To the memory of
Raymond Franz

CONTENTS

ACKNOWLEDGMENTS

IN MY first book, *The Reluctant Apostate*, I devoted several pages to naming the many dear people who have assisted me in my activism work over the years. Rather than name them all again, suffice it to say that I continue to be extremely grateful for their support, whether it is historic or ongoing.

Even so, I really should single out for special mention my immediate circle of friends and colleagues who, through their assistance and collaboration, make my work possible. The team at JWsurvey has been outstanding in their dedication and solidarity, namely Mark and Kimberly O'Donnell, Chloe Powell and "Covert Fade." Javier Ortiz, an honorary team member thanks to our collaboration on another important project (a documentary film titled *The Truth About the Truth*), has also been a reliable source of encouragement and guidance.

As far as the creation of this book is concerned, I need to acknowledge those who have directly helped in bringing it to life. Kyle Racki has designed a beautiful, attention-grabbing cover. Arthur Weber, who designed the layout and lovingly crafted each page, has applied the same care and scrupulous attention to detail that made *The Reluctant Apostate* so easy on the eye. Paul Grundy, one of two people who were instrumental in my own awakening (this book is dedicated to the memory of the other), has generously supplied a wonderful, very flattering foreword. And Graeme Hammond, Arthur Weber, Mark O'Donnell and "Covert

Fade" have all given me the benefit of their guidance, wisdom and expertise as editors.

I must also express my sincere appreciation to the following individuals, along with the many others who assisted with funding the publishing of this book via Indiegogo: Frank Jepsen, Ronald Feller, Ashley Latham, Barbara Weed, Sonia Mallet, William J. Fitten, Neil Buckley, Annette Davis, Kazimierz Walach, Annette Black, James A. Campbell, "Phoenix Seamstress," Malen Cross, Kelly Perazzolo, David Camilo, Joan M. Miller, Mark & Karla Wilmot, Derrick McCorkle, Philip Hickey, Jorian Micom, Kjetil Marius Waldersnes, "Luke Giles," Bea Gatchell, John Hutchinson, Sarah Harris, Erin Heald, Shaun Miller, Loretta Singhatat, Alex Reid and Andrew Blackman.

And finally, I need to give profound thanks to my loving wife Dijana for her unflinching affection, support and companionship. It is not always easy to surrender your spouse to intensive, emotionally draining work—especially when this occasionally attracts unwanted drama, resentment and controversy. Over the years, Dijana has become a true rock without whom it would be impossible to achieve a fraction of the activism work that has been accomplished, and for her incredible strength, understanding and love I will always be indebted.

AUTHOR'S NOTE

FOR ease of reading, I have mostly avoided citing references to quoted material in the main text. This information can instead be found in the "Notes" section at the end.

Please also note that I am not, and would never pretend to be, a therapist or any kind of authority on mental health. Nor would I presume to tell people how to live their lives. The advice offered in this book is merely based on what I have come to learn through my own experience and that of the many people who have contacted me over the years since I first started my activism.

This book is not intended as a psycho-educational tool. It is purely offered as a means of helping the reader navigate their way through the many challenges posed by leaving the Jehovah's Witness religion. As I explain in the pages to follow, if you feel distressed and traumatized by your exit from Jehovah's Witnesses, you would be well advised to seek the services of a qualified mental health professional who can advise you on techniques for coping with stress, anxiety and feelings of hopelessness, or who is able to prescribe further therapy or medication as needed.

FOREWORD

I FEEL honored to be writing the Foreword to such an important book. Leaving a high control religious group can be traumatic, particularly one that has control over your ability to associate with family and friends. The information contained within these pages will greatly assist in preparing the reader for what is to come, helping them make wise choices that will increase the likelihood of breaking free with minimal bad consequences.

Over the last two decades, it is estimated that well over two million Jehovah's Witnesses have left the Watchtower organization.[1] As revealed in the Pew Research Center's 2008 U.S. Religious Landscape Survey, Jehovah's Witnesses have the highest turnover of any religion in the United States, with two thirds of those raised as Witnesses eventually leaving. It is a tragedy that a religion with such a high turnover is also one of the most difficult to leave due to the excessive control wielded by the leadership. The organization's cruel policy of shunning former members makes it particularly difficult to acclimatize to life outside the Witness bubble without anyone by your side.

---

[1] This figure is derived from comparing the overall growth figures reported by Watchtower with the number of baptisms. For example, there was a shortfall of 1,529,060 publishers between 1996 and 2005. Even when we account for the mortality rate, this would indicate that well over one million Witnesses ceased participation in the preaching work over this period. For more information, please see my web page https://www.jwfacts.com/watchtower/statistics.php

In the past, many Witnesses were forced to leave without a support network and with limited access to information guiding them through the emotions and dilemmas they would encounter. Thankfully, the internet has now made this process considerably easier. However, to date there has been little in the way of specific advice of the kind outlined in this book, which summarizes the entire process in one comprehensive and well structured resource. I applaud Lloyd for taking the time to put together this information in an easy to read format.

Lloyd is a gifted writer, and through his activities has become a leading light in the ex-Jehovah's Witness community. I know from experience how taxing it is to be constantly involved with Watchtower activism; to be confronted by the heartbreaking stories emailed through from people who are frantically searching for advice. But Lloyd is driven by the same passion that consumes me— the desire to make a difference. As emotionally draining as this work can sometimes be, receiving messages of gratitude from those who have been able to move on with their lives having been positively affected by something I have written makes it all worth the effort.

Lloyd tells me that I was instrumental in helping him come to terms with discovering that Watchtower is not "the Truth," and I am proud that this is the case—especially given that he has gone on to play such an important role in assisting many more to reach that realization.

Having been raised as a Jehovah's Witness, and as someone who has been involved in helping people leave the religion for more than a decade, I have seen firsthand the tragic impact that it can have on people's lives. It would not be an exaggeration to say that the information in this book will save lives. In my experience, ceasing to be one of Jehovah's Witnesses has led to post-traumatic stress disorder, depression and, sadly, even suicide.

A guidebook that can highlight what to expect and the best way to approach leaving, while reminding the reader that the beautiful end result is always worth it, will surely prove invaluable. It offers the potential for readers to extract themselves with as few scars as possible, allowing them to go on to lead happier, more meaningful lives. I just hope that people are made aware of this resource as soon as they start having doubts about the organization so that they can plan their exit in an informed, measured way over a period of time, thus avoiding the many potential pitfalls.

One question that concerned me when I first launched jwfacts.com was whether I was doing people a favor by helping them realize that Watchtower does not teach "the Truth," particularly in view of the hardship people invariably go through when confronting this reality. But the email exchanges and online discussions that I have since had with those exiting have been overwhelmingly positive, convincing me that people are glad to have come to know "the truth about the truth," and are far happier and more content in their post-Watchtower lives. They do not regret their awakening. They do not yearn to continue living under delusion, no matter how reassuring it may seem to believe that you are one of God's chosen few, with the promise of eternal bliss in a paradise earth after surviving the destruction of the world.

I am now confident that those who escape Jehovah's Witnesses are better off in the long run. And it is reassuring for me to know that, from now on, there is a handbook that can make an otherwise perilous and traumatic journey that little bit easier for those leaving. I expect the exodus of Jehovah's Witnesses to continue to increase over the coming years. And I am sure the *Escape* book will become an invaluable tool in helping these ones move on as efficiently and painlessly as possible.

—Paul Grundy, author of JWfacts.com

INTRODUCTION

THIS book should not be needed. In the 21st century, a person should be free to decide that a certain religion is no longer for them and duly leave without fear of reprisals. Sadly, though, humanity still has a considerable way to go before freedom of conscience is truly honored across all cultures and creeds. Many abusive religious groups continue to exert a stranglehold on their members, and the men who lead Jehovah's Witnesses are no exception.

The Witness religion has been fairly described as a "captive organization."[1] Once a person is baptized as one of Jehovah's Witnesses, they are effectively locked into the movement for life. No allowance is made for lack of knowledge or maturity at the fateful point of immersion.

It matters not whether a Witness was baptized as young as eight—an age at which you are normally prevented by law from buying property, gaining employment or signing contracts.[2] Neither is any consideration given to the

---

[1] This wording was used by Senior Counsel Angus Stewart in his questioning of Governing Body member Geoffrey Jackson by video link on August 14, 2015 as part of Case Study 29 of the Australian government's Royal Commission into Institutional Responses to Child Sexual Abuse. Jackson was challenged on the policy of forcing believers, including abuse survivors, to choose between "freedom from the organization on the one hand and having to lose their family and friends and social network on the other." Stewart then asked, "Do you accept that putting people to that choice makes your organization in many respects a captive organization?" to which Jackson replied, "I do not accept that at all."

[2] The 2017 *Yearbook of Jehovah's Witnesses*, on page 26, includes the following message from a boy named Kodi: "Thanks for all the time

barrage of highly coercive indoctrination to which children of Jehovah's Witnesses are subjected, in many cases before they are even old enough to attend school.

A Witness may spend their childhood being inundated with extremely manipulative material in books, brochures, videos and cartoons. They may be urged to participate in coloring-in exercises, sing-along sessions, family worship evenings, long meetings and hours of door-to-door preaching—all geared toward encouraging their allegiance to the religion of their parents so that an eagerness to commit to the faith becomes almost inevitable. But sustained coercion from infancy is not allowed to count for anything when elders are deliberating the fate of someone who later decides that the religion is not for them.

Once the head dips beneath the water of the baptismal pool, the "faithful slave" will hold Witnesses to their decision *forever,* with family estrangement the ever-looming prospect for any who go back on their pledge. Only by "fading" into inactivity can an unbelieving Witness have a hope of evading punishment, with the caveat that he or she can never be open about their unbelief—essentially taking their doubts and troubles to the grave.[3]

Of course, you know all this, because this book is written for those who have spent considerable time in the Witness faith and have already resolved that they must leave, hav-

---

and effort you put into making jw.org, JW Broadcasting, and the Caleb and Sophia videos. Thank you for making the Bible easier to understand. I was baptized when I was eight. When I'm a bit older, I'm going to volunteer to help build Kingdom Halls! And I would like to work at Bethel. I'm nine now, so I've not got long to go."

[3] Even faders cannot be guaranteed a worry-free existence, as I will explain in a later chapter. Elders have been known to hunt down and disfellowship faders years or decades after they have stopped attending meetings on learning of their unbelief.

ing reached the conclusion that the theological claims of Watchtower are not as justified as they once assumed.

Perhaps you have had enough of the organization's appalling mishandling of cases of child abuse, or you have noticed that the shunning of disfellowshipped ones is cruel and unloving, or it could be that you simply can no longer nod along with Watchtower's convoluted and ever-changing Bible interpretations. After all, if the religion is not true there is no point wasting one more moment indulging in it no matter how benevolent or satisfying parts of it may be.

Regardless of how you reached the point of awakening from your indoctrination, it is very commendable that you have come this far in your journey. It takes enormous bravery to challenge dearly cherished beliefs, especially when you have years or decades of your life invested in promoting them. Many Witnesses will go to their graves without being able to summon the intellectual honesty that you are now demonstrating.

By sincerely and conscientiously striving to differentiate fact from fiction, reality from myth, truth from lie, you have put yourself on the road to freedom from a life that would otherwise almost certainly have been swallowed up in servitude to a heartless, unmerciful, self-serving, manipulative organization. You have gained a huge victory by freeing yourself mentally and emotionally from Watchtower's grip. But if you have sought out this book, it is likely because you feel much work is still ahead of you.

I initially contemplated titling this book "How to Leave Jehovah's Witnesses" but I soon realized that this title was inadequate because it did not properly reflect the challenges facing an awakened Witness. You do not simply *leave* the Jehovah's Witness religion, just as you cannot excuse yourself from a gang of thugs who are holding you against your will. You need to *escape* from it. Calculated resistance and careful planning are required, because the odds are stacked against you.

Ever since 1981, when Watchtower changed the rules so that disassociated ones were thenceforth to be punished the same as disfellowshipped ones by means of shunning, there has been no dignified way for a baptized Witness to part company with the organization for conscientious reasons.[4] Over the ensuing decades, the Watchtower organization has plunged deeper into an absolutist, black-and-white siege mentality whereby anyone who leaves must be feared and loathed. Their approach is: "If you are not for us, you must be against us!" A minefield of obstacles has therefore been carefully laid to block any attempts by would-be escapees who simply wish to move on with their lives with as little acrimony and unpleasantness as possible.

The good news is, you are by no means alone! Many have been through the situation you now face, myself included. I vividly remember the dizzying, sickening, hangover-like feeling of discovering that almost everything you have been taught (and have shared in teaching others) over many years is a lie.

I have faced the dilemma of whether to "fade" or walk away entirely through formal disassociation. I have locked

---

[4] It could be that you have been raised as a Jehovah's Witness but never actually baptized. If this is the case, your situation will be significantly easier because—though you can still be considered "bad association"—there is no formal requirement for believing family to shun you. Even so, I hope that reading this book will be a useful exercise for you, if only to remind you of the various complications and difficulties you have avoided by resisting any pressure to commit to the faith.

horns with elders who have been anxious to incriminate me, perplexed that anyone could seek to exit the organization unless they are a deplorable, conniving sinner. As someone who has trodden the road ahead of you it will be my responsibility in the following pages to be your guide—a companion who will help you navigate the obstacles with confidence.

Obviously, it is virtually impossible for me to anticipate every situation you might face. Everyone's circumstances will be different, and there may be some difficulties facing you that I cannot envision or relate to. But there are many hurdles facing all awakened Witnesses that, due to the organization's strict unity and adherence to clearly defined policies, will be almost identical.

For example, having been an elder myself, I can tell you what moves to expect from your elders in their efforts to frustrate your escape. I can help you prepare for the inevitable attempts at salvaging your loyalty to the "faithful slave" and bringing you back to the "flock." I can, and will, walk you through what to say—and what not to say—if your elders begin interfering, perhaps with the aim of launching judicial action against you.

Perhaps you are worried about how your family will respond as they notice you distancing yourself. Having experienced firsthand the awkwardness and stress of dealing with believing family members, including a wife who was initially horrified to see my faith evaporate, I can give you the benefit of what I have learned.

More than anything, I hope that by reading this book you will understand that the process you are going through is common and that many have traversed the road that now stretches ahead of you. Despite seemingly insurmountable obstacles, including emotional upheaval and family estrangement, they have forged happy, meaningful lives for themselves. Though once they may have been unquestioning followers of the "slave," on a never-ending hamster wheel of trying to live up to impossible expectations, they are now living authentic lives in which they are free to be true to themselves, surrounded by those who love and value them for who they are.

Freedom is the real paradise that lies ahead of you, and it is far more rewarding than empty promises of frolicking with pandas and feasting at fruit-filled picnic tables. In the following pages, we will examine ways of getting you to your destination as painlessly as possible. Together, we will plot your escape!

CHAPTER ONE

"LORD, WHOM SHALL WE GO AWAY TO?"

THE words forming the title to this chapter will be very familiar to you if you have spent any time as one of Jehovah's Witnesses. They are recorded as having been spoken by the apostle Peter at John chapter six.

Jesus had just caused outrage by recommending that people feed on his flesh and drink his blood (symbolically, we can assume!). His audience at the synagogue balked at the macabre, cannibalistic tone, saying: "This speech is shocking; who can listen to it?" Even many of his disciples, we are told, "went off to the things behind and would no longer walk with him."

Turning to his most loyal followers, the "Twelve," Jesus asked whether they too would be deserting him. Peter, presumably answering on behalf of all of them, is recorded as saying: "Lord, whom shall we go away to? You have sayings of everlasting life. We have believed and have come to know that you are the Holy One of God." —John 6:60-69

Jehovah's Witnesses are urged to consider this exchange whenever doubts surface as to whether their beliefs are true. "Jehovah's spirit and blessings are linked to the one association of brothers that God is using," says one *Watchtower* magazine. "Even if someone in the congregation upsets us, where else can we turn? Nowhere else can we hear the sayings of everlasting life." Commenting on the same verse, another *Watchtower* remarks:

> By cutting off association with Christ and his faithful followers, [disciples who abandoned Jesus] lost their spirituality and their joy. Have those who stopped associating with the Christian congregation found another place where there is rich spiritual food? No, for there is none!

A black-and-white dilemma is thus presented where you, as a Witness, face two possibilities: associate with the one true "Christian congregation" as someone who embraces its teachings, or depart into despair, darkness and futility.

Only once you shed the assumption that Jehovah's Witnesses are "the one association of brothers that God is using" does it become clear that the account in question has no bearing on someone who has come to sincerely doubt their Witness beliefs. We can choose between two arguments for anyone who insists otherwise: the Christian argument, and the atheist argument.[1]

If you are a believer in Christianity, you can retort that rejecting Jehovah's Witnesses need not mean one is rejecting Christ. Peter would have been turning his back on Jesus himself—not a New York-based group of leaders claiming his sole approval. One is reminded of the words at Matthew 7:21-23:

---

[1] Though I am an atheist, I will endeavor to write this book for both believers and non-believers without unduly insisting that people join me in my unbelief. After all, it makes little difference to me whether you decide to hold on to belief in God or reject it. I only recommend that you consider both as options, since it is possible to live a happy, meaningful, moral, even spiritual life whether you acknowledge a creator or not.

> "Not everyone saying to me, 'Lord, Lord,' will enter into the Kingdom of the heavens, but only the one doing the will of my Father who is in the heavens will. Many will say to me in that day: 'Lord, Lord, did we not prophesy in your name, and expel demons in your name, and perform many powerful works in your name?' And then I will declare to them: 'I never knew you! Get away from me, you workers of lawlessness!'"

We also have the words at Deuteronomy 18:20-22 to consider, which are uncannily prescient in the context of a group notorious for its string of false predictions[2] in God's name:

> If any prophet presumptuously speaks a word in my name that I did not command him to speak or speaks in the name of other gods, that prophet must die. However, you may say in your heart: "How will we know that Jehovah has not spoken the word?" When the prophet speaks in the name of Jehovah and the word is not fulfilled or does not come true, then Jehovah did not speak that word. The prophet spoke it presumptuously. You should not fear him.

There is thus no reason to fear Watchtower or be intimidated by their efforts to manipulate you into staying with them regardless of your doubts and concerns. The organization has a reputation of consistent failure as prophets, not to mention a track record of double standards, incompetence, lies and abuse. If, despite all this, Watchtower insists that following the Governing Body is the same as following Jesus, it is incumbent on them to

---

[2] Watchtower apologists will often reply that this verse cannot be applied to Jehovah's Witnesses, because the organization has never claimed to act as a prophet. For an excellent rebuttal to this argument, I recommend the following web page: https://jwfacts.com/watchtower/jehovahs-prophet.php

present proof of their divine mandate, which they have never come close to doing.[3]

Like any professed Christian denomination, Watchtower can only *claim* exclusivity as God's one true faith and hope that sufficient numbers of people can be persuaded. But the simple truth is: you can reject the Jehovah's Witness religion and still call yourself a Christian. In fact, the overwhelming majority of Christians do precisely this! As former Governing Body member Raymond Franz put it:

> I feel no need to "go" anywhere. For I know the One who has the "sayings of everlasting life." I appreciate the strengthening companionship of those I have with whom to associate (either personally or by correspondence) and hope that the future will add to my acquaintance with yet other sincere persons whose concern is for truth, not simply in doctrine, in words, but as a way of life.

Then there is the atheist argument, which is that the conversation with Peter cannot be proven to have happened in the first place, and therefore there is little point agonizing over its meaning—especially if we are talking about a meaning asserted by one of the countless Christian denominations throughout history that have claimed a monopoly on interpreting scripture.

The Gospels contain many uplifting stories (my own favorite is that of the good Samaritan) but, on close inspection, they are also riddled with inconsistencies when com-

---

[3] As you will know, Witnesses are taught that early Watchtower leaders received their commission as the "faithful and discreet slave" in 1919 following a period of inspection and cleansing by Jesus. Obviously, this is an unfalsifiable theological claim of the kind indulged in by any number of religions. Do we conclude that Joseph Smith, founder of the Mormon faith, discovered golden plates laden with divine revelations simply because he said so?

pared to each other. This would indicate that, rather than forming a reliable historical narrative, they are more likely a product of the imaginations of unknown writers. Indeed, considering the extraordinary influence the New Testament has had on the last two millennia of world history, it can be sobering to ponder just how little we know about where it has come from. As Simon Loveday observes in his excellent book *The Bible for Grown-Ups*:

> Paradoxically, we know more about those who wrote the Old Testament than we do about those who wrote the New Testament.

Loveday goes on to explain:

> We know extraordinarily little about the four evangelists, the people who wrote the first surviving accounts of Jesus. We do not know their names: the original Gospels do not bear an author's name, and Matthew, Mark, Luke, and John are all merely guesses added 50 years or more after the books were first written and circulated. We do not know where they lived (though it was almost certainly outside Judea). We do not know their sex: it is unlikely that any was a woman, but women do feature largely in all four Gospels, notably in Luke. We do not even know for sure whether the writers were Jews or Gentiles.

Whether you are a believer or an unbeliever, however, it is not always as straightforward as simply applying cold, hard logic to dubious claims and flawed reasoning. You may be fully comfortable in knowing that you are not rejecting Jesus or foolishly foregoing some promise of eternal life, but if the words in John chapter six have been drilled into you over many years, perhaps even since you were a young child, you can still find yourself beset by "what ifs": "But what if I'm overlooking something? What if I have allowed myself to arrogantly rely on my own reasoning, and by doing so I am throwing away something precious—something eternal?"

Cult indoctrination is never to be underestimated.[4] Given sufficient repetition, even the most ludicrous, far-fetched ideas can be extremely persistent and may linger in your mind long after you have consciously rejected them— especially if they are backed up with emotional reasoning ("If you don't believe this, then you are betraying your family and God himself!") or threats and fear-mongering ("If you don't believe this, then you will be among those slaughtered at Armageddon!"). It is for this reason that I cannot stress enough the need for you to expect doubts and flashbacks during your bid for freedom.

If you get to the end of this book and *still* suffer with moments of fear, panic and uncertainty over your decision to part with the Jehovah's Witness faith, don't despair! It is perfectly normal to struggle with such thoughts long after you have convinced yourself that you were lied to.

As a former believer myself, I have been writing and speaking publicly about the Witness faith for a number of years—and even I have fleeting moments of uncertainty and introspection! Granted, these episodes are becoming more scarce as the years pass since my official exit in 2013. But if even the author of this book must occasionally deal with flutterings of doubt, there is every reason for you to

---

[4] I will be unapologetically referring to Jehovah's Witnesses as a cult in this book, because it is written for people who have, through personal experience, come to view this as a fair character-ization of the Witness faith and wish to do something about it. If you are reading this as someone who has yet to be convinced that the movement is a cult, please refer to my first book, *The Reluctant Apostate*, in which I explain my reasons for using this word in more detail.

expect the same if you are only just beginning the process of breaking free.

When confronted by such thoughts, I find I can rely on a simple mental exercise that is guaranteed to steady my nerves and alleviate nagging doubts. This method forms the basis of the next chapter, and it is arguably the most crucial tool in the arsenal of any escapee from Watchtower doctrine. It is the "three R's": ***Research, Research, Research!***

As Chapter Two will shortly demonstrate in more detail, nothing eviscerates deeply ingrained falsehood and flawed argumentation like the searing light of logic, reason and fact-based information. If doubts and flashbacks are mounting an insurgency in your mind, then your mind is the battlefield where these must be engaged and dealt with.

By calling in "backup" in the form of books, videos and blog articles dealing with the specific areas of uncertainty, you can reassure yourself that you are on the right track and have confidence that your decision to walk away from Jehovah's Witnesses is sound and justified. Watchtower may have succeeded in planting disturbing, unsettling ideas so deep in your mind that it is impossible to fully purge them, but at least by reminding yourself of why and how you have been manipulated and misinformed you can keep these hang-ups contained and in check.

This, by the way, is far from how you would deal with doubts as a Jehovah's Witness. In Watchtower literature, Witnesses who struggle with doubts are urged to pursue a three-fold solution. They are to pray, do research about the subject of their doubts using only Watchtower publications and, if all else fails (as it usually will), they must "wait on Jehovah"—effectively burying their heads in the sand, having faith that Jehovah's "faithful slave" knows best. As a 1996 *Watchtower* article advised:

> What if we individually have difficulty understand-
> ing or accepting a certain point? We should pray for
> wisdom and undertake research in the Scriptures and
> Christian publications. (Proverbs 2:4, 5; James 1:5-8)
> Discussion with an elder may help. If the point still
> cannot be understood, it may be best to let the matter
> rest. Perhaps more information on the subject will be
> published, and then our understanding will be broad-
> ened. It would be wrong, however, to try to convince
> others in the congregation to accept our own divergent
> opinion. This would be sowing discord, not working to
> preserve unity. How much better it is to "go on walking
> in the truth" and encourage others to do so!—3 John 4.

Hence, when doubts creep into the mind of a Jehovah's Witness, the solution is to suspend disbelief and assume that Watchtower—supposedly God's one true spirit-di-rected organization—could never err in its teachings or theological claims. Only one side of the argument can be heard and anything critical of the organization must be strenuously ignored. Any Witness who discovers something that threatens to "sow discord" by debunking previously es-tablished dogma must practice self-censorship and persist with encouraging total strangers to believe things of which they themselves are uncertain.

But once you have freed yourself from fear of Watch-tower and you find yourself questioning your decision to leave, the solution is far more satisfying. You are free to fully explore both sides of the argument through meaning-ful, objective research, unafraid of what you will discover. Hence, you might ask: "What is the specific belief or teach-ing that is troubling me?" Having identified what it is, you could then ask: "What have I been persuaded to believe by Watchtower and what do Watchtower publications say on this matter? What do other sources (critics, historians, Bible scholars, scientists) say on this matter? Does this teaching make sound, logical sense? How does this teaching stand up to what I know to be objectively true?"

As Witnesses, we were taught to fear doubts and eradicate them whenever they surfaced. As ex-Witnesses, we can teach ourselves to embrace skepticism, acknowledging that we do not have all the answers to life's questions and most likely never will. Yes, doubts can be unpleasant if they are based on coercion and misinformation or they are making us feel guilty or unworthy, but once wrestled into their proper place through the application of logic and reason they can also be a valuable, intimate reminder of how much we have advanced and matured.

Doubts may still pester us from time to time, but the more our mind is equipped with knowledge and argumentation derived by means of proper research and logical, coherent reasoning, the less troubling and more fleeting these episodes of uncertainty are likely to be. The moment we do not have any doubts and feel completely confident that we know everything is arguably the moment we need to panic, because it is likely that we have fallen under the spell of another cult!

Having identified research as a crucial component in the process of exiting Watchtower's influence, we can now examine resources that will help us in keeping doubts at bay, allowing us to wield this vital tool as effectively as possible. But regardless of what your religious (or non-religious) beliefs end up being after walking away from Jehovah's Witnesses, let nobody persuade you that you are giving up on "everlasting life" by escaping Watchtower.

Whether you are religious or not, life is a precious and extremely rare gift and we cannot afford to waste a moment of it believing and expounding bad ideas. When asked for an answer to "Lord, whom shall we go away to?" my answer is: "I'm going nowhere. I'm getting rid of lies and wrong assumptions, and I'm much happier and less confused by so doing!"

CHAPTER TWO

RESEARCH, RESEARCH, RESEARCH!

JEHOVAH'S WITNESSES are not dissuaded from doing research. All Witnesses are urged to make a habit of "personal study" sessions, which include meditating on Bible verses. If a Witness happens to be a male and is therefore eligible for congregation speaking assignments, they may find extra incentives to do research. If a brother climbs on the platform to deliver an assigned talk without having prepared well in advance, this will soon become noticeable.

Whether male or female, Witnesses will generally feel guilty if they arrive for a meeting without having fastidiously combed through the material under discussion. In the era before tablets were widely used in Kingdom Halls, this was usually done by means of brightly-colored highlighter pens—a helpful indicator signaling to other Witnesses (who may be glancing over one's shoulder) that the material had been properly studied!

But, as you know, this "research" is mostly limited to the Bible and Watchtower publications, either in hard copies (in your personal collection or at the Kingdom Hall library) or in digital form such as via the *Watchtower Library* software, the *JW Library* phone app, or the *Watchtower ONLINE LIBRARY* web pages. When it comes to understanding spiritual matters, external sources are not recommended. As a 1997 *Watchtower* remarked:

The publications and research tools provided by Jehovah's organization stimulate our minds with upbuilding thoughts and train us to distinguish right from wrong. (Hebrews 5:14) We should cling to these provisions as we would to a raft in a turbulent sea.

A 1996 *Our Kingdom Ministry* was even more explicit in singling out Watchtower publications as the only reliable source of information:

> Our lives depend on spiritual food from Jehovah. (Matt. 4:4) Those who look to worldly sources for spiritual sustenance go hungry while we eat and drink to satisfaction. (Isa. 65:13) The 'faithful slave' gives us access to an inexhaustible supply of knowledge that leads to everlasting life.—Matt. 24:45; John 17:3.

What if, having consulted only Watchtower publications for "spiritual sustenance," you have a question that has not been satisfactorily answered? Does a Witness then have permission to consult "worldly sources?" A 2011 *Watchtower* was happy to clarify:

> Of course, there are some topics and scriptures that our publications have not specifically addressed. And even where we have commented on a particular Bible text, we may not have dealt with the specific question that you have in mind. Also, some Bible accounts raise questions because not all the details are spelled out in the Scriptures. Thus, we cannot find immediate answers to every question that arises. In such a case, we should avoid speculating about things that simply cannot be answered, lest we get involved in debating "questions for research rather than a dispensing of anything by God in connection with faith." (1 Tim. 1:4; 2 Tim. 2:23; Titus 3:9) Neither the branch office nor world headquarters is in a position to analyze and answer all such questions that have not been considered in our

literature. We can be satisfied that the Bible provides sufficient information to guide us through life but also omits enough details so as to require us to have strong faith in its divine Author.—See pages 185 to 187 of the book *Draw Close to Jehovah*.

Hence, if you have a question that is not answered in Watchtower publications, there must be something wrong with the question! Jehovah has caused all proper, reasonable questions to be answered in the Bible and through the "faithful slave." Anything 'omitted' from these sources is not worth worrying about and should be regarded as an opportunity for you to show extra faith. And do not assume that you can write the headquarters for an answer, because they are 'not in a position' to help you! You must continue to be content with using Watchtower publications—and *only* Watchtower publications—for your research.

The reasoning on show here is manifestly ludicrous. Think, for a moment, what you can expect to learn if you rely *solely* on information that is produced by a religious movement claiming to be God's only channel of spiritual food for mankind. Can the information you are consulting be considered objective? Is there any incentive for the writers to criticize their organization whenever criticism is warranted (as will inevitably be the case) or is it more likely that criticism will be suppressed by such an organization, while its achievements are grossly exaggerated?

Once any group can bring itself to make the fantastic claim that it is exclusively a conduit for divine wisdom, how, realistically, could it then admit that it is in error even when this proves to be the case? Would not the entire premise of divine guidance be seriously undermined by even one apology or admission of guilt? After all, if God is really using this group, why would he influence it to act wrongly or propagate myth?

I realize I am in danger of stating the glaringly obvious when I point out that no religious movement claiming divine authority will ever admit that it is wrong, but this point must be especially stressed when we are dealing with Watchtower and its efforts to control Jehovah's Witnesses. Why? Because over many decades the organization has mastered the art, not just of glossing over the flaws in its literature, but of convincing Witnesses that material from former believers exposing its mistakes and refuting its claims is dangerous and even *deadly*. Take, for example, these words from a 1992 *Watchtower*:

> Apostates capitalize on errors or sceming mistakes made by brothers who take the lead. Our safety lies in avoiding apostate propaganda as though it were poison, which in fact it is.

A 2006 *Watchtower* was similarly scathing:

> Do what God requires of you, and never consider partaking of "the table of demons." (1 Corinthians 10:21) Reject apostasy. Partake appreciatively of the spiritual food available only at Jehovah's table, and you will not be misled by false teachers or wicked spirit forces. (Ephesians 6:12; Jude 3, 4)

More recently, in 2011, Watchtower went so far as to question the mental health of former believers:

> Suppose that a doctor told you to avoid contact with someone who is infected with a contagious, deadly disease. You would know what the doctor means, and you would strictly heed his warning. Well, apostates are "mentally diseased," and they seek to infect others with their disloyal teachings. (1 Tim. 6:3, 4) Jehovah, the Great Physician, tells us to avoid contact with them. We

know what he means, but are we determined to heed his warning in all respects?

An image of apostates as the very worst of humanity is therefore conjured in the minds of Witnesses. Apostates are to be thought of as liars in league with Satan; pawns of "wicked spirit forces" who leap on the slightest mistakes, even stooping to fabricating damning information in their efforts to deceive. They are portrayed as disease-ridden, deranged con artists whose maniacal, corrosive attitudes can be infectious unless carefully avoided.

All of this paranoia, stigmatization and loathing has a powerful effect on Jehovah's Witnesses. It can make them terrified of the very idea of consulting an apostate source. I vividly recall the first time I made a conscious effort to discover what arguments might be found on an "apostate" website, and it was not a remotely pleasurable experience.

The genuine fear of displeasing God was palpable. My heart raced. I half expected a bolt of lightning to explode through the ceiling and render me a smoldering heap of ash. These acute feelings of trepidation and guilt were the direct result of repeated exposure since childhood to material such as that quoted above. Once you have become convinced that an organization is being used by God to dispense his one and only "Truth," you take its exhortations very seriously and assume any warnings about former members-turned-critics are justified and for your benefit.

Only once you shed the assumption that the organization speaks for God, and consciously give yourself permission to examine the other side of the argument, can you grasp that Watchtower's use of the word "apostate" is a clever use of language designed to make former members seem evil and sinister. When you consult the English dictionary, you find that an apostate is merely someone who walks away from his or her religion. Hence, you can be an apostate of Jehovah's Witnesses, Mormonism, Catholicism, Islam, Scientology, or any religious group you care to mention.

After all, what is so intrinsically wicked about turning your back on beliefs that you have genuinely determined to be false? Is it not wise, indeed incumbent on you, to pursue a course of intellectual honesty by distancing yourself from proven falsehood? Does not Watchtower itself acknowledge that it is prudent for new converts to forsake former beliefs they have discovered to be false, to the point of requiring the severing of all ties to former religions?[1] Rather than being a reason for shame, becoming an apostate should really be a source of pride if the apostate is excusing themselves for sincere, conscientious reasons. This is especially so if he or she must courageously overcome significant obstacles in the form of shunning and family estrangement to make such a stand.

Then there is the claim that apostates lie and are guilty of propaganda. This argument assumes that it is impossible for a Witness to abandon the organization without mutating into a dishonest individual bent on deceit and manipulation. It is also a sweeping generalization—an attempt at lumping all apostates together under one smear

---

[1] The book *Organized to Do Jehovah's Will* (2015 edition) insists on the following requirement for all unbaptized publishers (those who want to join in preaching with the congregation before getting baptized): "He has definitely broken off membership in all false religious organizations with which he may have been affiliated. He has ceased attending their services and sharing in or supporting their activities.—2 Cor. 6:14-18; Rev. 18:4."

in the hope that Witnesses will be put off from ever seeing for themselves whether there is any truth to be found in apostate sources.

In reality, though some apostate websites and You-Tube channels do indulge in exaggerated claims and can sometimes be fast and loose with the facts, the majority of apostate activists are keen to distance themselves from Watchtower's stereotype as much as possible, and will fastidiously quote references in support of their arguments so that their audience can be assured of their honesty and diligence. Moreover, the ex-JW "community" is known for valuing skepticism, and activists who routinely try to deceive people or invent ridiculous, far-fetched stories about Watchtower tend to find themselves scorned and discredited.

As to apostates being accused of propaganda, this is a rather obvious case of Watchtower pointing the finger where two fingers must be pointed straight back. Consider, for example, the following quote from a 2017 *Watchtower*:

> Keep in mind that Satan does not want you to think clearly or reason things out well. Why? Because propaganda "is likely to be most effective," says one source, "if people . . . are discouraged from thinking critically." (*Media and Society in the Twentieth Century*) So never be content passively or blindly to accept what you hear. (Prov. 14:15) Use your God-given thinking abilities and power of reason to make the truth your own.—Prov. 2:10-15; Rom. 12:1, 2.

In a supreme irony, if Lyn Gorman and David McLean's *Media and Society in the Twentieth Century* is consulted directly, it becomes apparent that Watchtower is guilty of disingenuously omitting part of the quote that condemns the organization's approach to apostate sources. The un-doc-tored quote reads (the omitted text is in bold):

> Therefore, it is likely to be most effective if people **do not have access to multiple sources of information and if they** are discouraged from thinking critically. Michael Balfour has suggested that the best touchstone for distinguishing propaganda from science is whether a plurality of sources of information and interpretations is being discouraged or fostered.

By actively dissuading followers from consulting apostate sources to deliberate their truthfulness, Watchtower incriminates itself as the very worst kind of propagandist—one that controls people by limiting access to information.

You would think an organization claiming to be custodians of God's one and only "Truth" would be undaunted at the prospect of its members consulting contradictory sources of information. They might even savor the prospect of Witnesses strengthening their faith by seeing for themselves how manifestly fallacious such sources are. Instead, Watchtower's repeated berating of apostates and insistence on Witnesses ignoring their arguments betrays an underlying insecurity and a readiness to deceive and manipulate in furtherance of its agenda.[2]

It should also be noted that propaganda need not be deceptive in and of itself. The *Oxford English Dictionary*

---

[2] As you may be aware, Watchtower goes so far as to make allowances for Witnesses to act dishonestly when doing so benefits the organization—a strategy known as "theocratic warfare." A 1960 *Watchtower* commented: "As a soldier of Christ [the Christian] is in theocratic warfare and he must exercise added caution when dealing with God's foes. Thus the Scriptures show that for the purpose of protecting the interests of God's cause, it is proper to hide the truth from God's enemies."

defines propaganda as "information, especially of a biased or misleading nature, used to promote a political cause or point of view." It is quite possible to be biased toward a political cause or point of view that is noble and benign, and to seek to influence others to embrace your cause by spreading information in support of it. Any printed material, videos, "tweets" or Facebook posts that you share or disseminate could be thought of as propaganda, but if your cause is objectively beneficial and just (e.g. furthering human rights or promoting environmental awareness) nobody could reasonably take issue with the motives behind your "propaganda" campaign.

Furthermore, if you are convinced that your cause is advantageous and defensible, you would not be falling over yourself to urge people to ignore the other side of the debate. You would be happy to let your arguments stand on their own merits, possibly even welcoming opposing viewpoints to more clearly highlight the merits of your position and the unreasonableness of your opponents.

When you review apostate "propaganda," you overwhelmingly find that, contrary to Watchtower's propaganda, *both sides* of the argument are presented and you are actively encouraged to reach your own conclusions based on the facts.

While Watchtower's digital resources (mentioned above) only offer you publications going back a few decades, there are apostate websites with downloadable Watchtower publications going all the way back to the very beginning of the organization. Why? Because, as it turns out, there is no better means of highlighting the false predictions, flip-flops, fanciful conjecture, flawed arguments and misinformation disseminated by the "faithful slave" over many decades than consulting the very writings in which these are to be found.

At this point, a devout Witness might retort: "Ah, but publications from the days of Russell and Rutherford are old light. They are no longer relevant to Witness theology and teachings because we have moved on spiritually and organizationally since those days."

Firstly, the early beginnings of "Jehovah's organization" are hardly irrelevant if it was during this era that God singled out Watchtower as his chosen channel with mankind. For example, you might consider the 1917 book *The Finished Mystery* to be an obsolete relic from a bygone era when the organization was ignorant and unenlightened. Certainly, the book itself brims with fanciful and embarrassing assertions and conjecture—as is immediately evident to anyone who has tracked down a copy and leafed through its pages. However, is not Jesus said to have inspected and cleansed his "spiritual temple" between 1914 and 1919—a process that resulted in Watchtower being selected over all the other religious groups of the period?

Given that *The Finished Mystery* was published in 1917— right in the middle of Jesus' cleansing and inspection process—does not its message carry a unique significance? Similarly, once senior Watchtower officials had been selected as God's "faithful slave," are there not basic expectations that we can reasonably apply to Watchtower materials printed from 1919 onward? Can we not anticipate rudimentary standards of honesty, transparency and rationality from the organization over this period? And where else will we find evidence along these lines than in the material the organization was busily printing and distributing—irrespective of how bright the "light" was back then?

Secondly, Witness apologists would do well to meditate on the entire concept of "new light" versus "old light." When you consult the scriptures used by Watchtower to justify this teaching (namely, the teaching that God progressively reveals scriptural truth to Christians over many decades) you find that none of these describe a scenario in which God would willfully and deliberately convey falsehood to his worshippers as a makeweight until actual truth is divulged at a later time.[3]

There are two important questions a Witness should be asking in this regard: "Is God guiding the Watchtower organization by means of his holy spirit, including the teachings and theology conveyed in Watchtower publications?" and "Is God capable of lying, even if on an ends-justify-means basis?"[4]

Either Jehovah lies or he does not. If he does not lie, then (if you are a believer) it is blasphemous for you to suggest that God influenced the early organization to write falsehood as a surrogate for truth—a truth that was only to be revealed in later decades.

Truth, you see, is truth. There is no such thing as "present truth," no matter what any group of religious leaders will tell you. If Watchtower claims Jehovah's guidance while acknowledging that its previous teachings were in error, it is essentially blaming Jehovah for these errors.

Once you have overcome these or any other hang-ups about apostate "propaganda," and you accept that older Watchtower publications are a valid testing ground for the

---

[3] I go through some of the various verses used by Watchtower in defense of its "new light" teaching in my 2013 video on the John Cedars channel, *Debunking "Increasing Light" in Less Than 8 Minutes!*

[4] Titus 1:2 might prove useful in answering this second question.

lofty theological claims of the "faithful slave," a rich, fertile pasture of fascinating and revealing resources opens up before you, inviting you to gorge on meaningful, satisfying, *objective* research. You may even find yourself learning so much about the Jehovah's Witness religion that you eventually know more than the average elder, and you will be baffled at how such knowledge could have been so effectively withheld from you for so long using little more than threats, intimidation and fear!

Having explained the value of research and the reasons why we can dismiss Watchtower's efforts to restrict it, I will devote the remaining pages of this chapter to listing some of the research tools I have personally discovered to be helpful, and share pointers on what you can expect to find therein.

WATCHTOWER PUBLICATIONS

Watchtower materials dating back to the days of Charles Taze Russell can be relatively easy to locate if you know where to look. Here follows a list of online resources where older books, booklets and magazines can be found if you are not keen on hunting them down in thrift stores or on eBay.[5]

AvoidJW.org has compiled a comprehensive selection of downloadable publications dating all the way back to

---

[5] As an ex-Witness writer and activist, I have been able to assemble my own extensive collection of Watchtower materials going back to the Russell era, mostly thanks to the enormous generosity of my supporters who have donated books to me. If you do a search for Watchtower books on eBay, you may be astonished at some of the prices depending on how old or rare a certain item is. It is not uncommon for a book or booklet printed during the presidency of Russell or Rutherford to fetch hundreds or even thousands of dollars.

the beginning of the organization, including elder letters and guidebooks that rank-and-file publishers are prohibited from accessing. The vast majority of this meticulously organized trove of copyrighted material, though directly relevant to Witness beliefs, teachings and policies, would be almost impossible to consult if not somehow made available online.[6]

WatchtowerWayback.org offers a similar service, with materials available for download in both French and English.

archive.org is a non-profit online library (not maintained by ex-Witnesses) that can also be used to access older Watchtower materials. The pages are a little more confusing to navigate, but if you spend some time familiarizing yourself with how the website works you may be able to locate the PDF you are looking for. (Familiarity with the literature abbreviations in the *Watch Tower Publications Index* may also prove advantageous.)

---

[6] As reported by the Irish newspaper *The Sunday Business Post* (January 28-29, 2018), Watchtower has gone so far as to apply for a DMCA subpoena against AvoidJW.org in an attempt to "shut down the blog" for distributing its copyrighted content. The article reports that Watchtower sought the subpoena "to force search engine Google and web hosting company GoDaddy to provide the Jehovah's Witnesses with customer account contact information, contact information for the domain, any related email accounts, and log files for the WordPress account." One has to wonder: if senior Watchtower officials genuinely believe the organization's writings represent "spiritual food" that must be spread far and wide on a without-charge basis, should they not be thanking those who facilitate this rather than pursuing legal action against them—even to the point of trying to learn who has accessed the information? Disturbingly, it seems the action against AvoidJW.org may be part of a broader strategy. The organization has indicated in the April 2018 study edition of *The Watchtower* that it will pursue through the courts those who "try to use our publications on their websites to lure in Jehovah's Witnesses and others."

Ex-Witness Books

Crisis of Conscience is arguably the must-read book for exiting Jehovah's Witnesses, as it offers an unparalleled behind-the-scenes glimpse at Watchtower's inner workings. Raymond Franz—nephew of one-time Watchtower president Fred Franz—was a Governing Body member for nearly a decade, over which period he witnessed firsthand the bickering, blunders and power struggles at the pinnacle of the organization's hierarchy.

Clearly mindful of the need to back up his claims and arguments with evidence, Franz was careful to supply scans of key correspondence and quotes from literature wherever this was called for. The overall result is a precious resource that has already helped generations of Witnesses to find freedom from Watchtower, and I believe it will continue to assist and inspire generations to come.

In Search of Christian Freedom is Raymond Franz's follow-up book in which he delves into Witness doctrine in more detail, with less emphasis on his personal story. The overriding message is that it is possible to maintain a personal Christian faith without subjugating oneself to Watchtower's organizationally oriented belief system.

The Reluctant Apostate, written by yours truly (full disclosure!), is a blend of personal memoir and in-depth discussion of Watchtower teachings and history from the organization's beginnings right the way up to recent times. I wrote the book primarily for a non-Witness audience, requiring me to adopt an expositional style. However, I have tried to cater as much as possible to current and former Witness readers. For example, inserted in the text at appropriate points are "For Witnesses" boxes, in which I directly address the Witness reader on a particular topic, such as disfellowshipping, blood transfusions, or the subjection of women.

Apocalypse Delayed, by M. James Penton, is arguably the definitive reference work when it comes to understanding Watchtower history and the gradual development of the religion's theology. Penton is a professor emeritus of history at the University of Lethbridge in Alberta, Canada, and he brings his scholarly approach to bear on his former religion with this extremely helpful work. I have personally found Penton's recounting of Watchtower history from Russell's founding of the Bible Student movement through to the Rutherford years to be extremely enlightening in my efforts to better understand the organization's origins.[7]

The Gentile Times Reconsidered, by Carl Olof Jonsson, focuses attention on Watchtower's insistence on 607 B.C.E. as the date of Jerusalem's destruction by the Babylonian armies under Nebuchadnezzar. Jonsson takes the reader through multiple lines of compelling evidence that thoroughly debunks the organization's claim, so crucial to its theology, that 1914 was a year marked in Bible prophecy.

Exiting the JW Cult: A Healing Handbook for Current & Former Jehovah's Witnesses is the first of several highly-recommended books by Bonnie Zieman.[8] Zieman draws from

[7] If, like me, you share a fascination with Joseph Rutherford and the extent to which the "Judge" moulded the Watchtower organization in his image, I would also strongly recommend Penton's *Jehovah's Witnesses and the Third Reich: Sectarian Politics under Persecution*. Penton is arguably the foremost scholar on Watchtower history. It was my pleasure to interview him for my YouTube channel in 2018.

[8] I had the pleasure of interviewing Zieman in 2017 in a video that should be easily found in the YouTube search feature. Her recent titles include *Fading Out of the JW Cult: A Memoir, The Challenge to Heal Workbook & Journal: Work Out & Release Trauma Resulting*

her Witness background, combined with her training and experience as a licensed psychotherapist, to provide an invaluable handbook for those seeking to heal from the emotional wounds inflicted by the organization and its teachings.

Combating Cult Mind Control, by Steven Hassan, is not an ex-Witness book,[9] but it very clearly identifies and explains the mechanisms used by the leaders of various cults—including Jehovah's Witnesses—to exploit and control people. Hassan's BITE model, in particular, is a very useful tool for understanding how cults successfully influence their followers.

These are by no means the only books dealing with Watchtower history and teachings—there are many, many others by various authors stretching back decades—but the above titles immediately spring to mind if I am recommending tools for research.

Ex-Witness memoirs can also provide a fascinating insight into the human cost of Watchtower dogma. Books like Richard Kelly's *Growing Up in Mama's Club,* Scott Terry's *Cowboys, Armageddon, and the Truth* and Debbie McDaniel's *Out With Consequences* are all excellent resources for better understanding how far-reaching and impactful the Witness faith can be on a personal level.

Ex-Witness Websites

JWfacts.com is a superb online resource for researching the

from *High-Control Situations, The Challenge to Heal: After Leaving a High-Control Group* and *Cracking the Cult Code for Therapists: What Every Cult Victim Wants Their Therapist to Know.*

[9] Hassan draws on his experience in the Moonies (the Unification Church) as inspiration for his work in helping raise awareness of cults.

beliefs, teachings and history of Jehovah's Witnesses. Paul Grundy (who kindly supplied the foreword!) is the author and founder, and he has organized a number of carefully-researched and well-written essays so that you can easily navigate topic by topic, focusing on the issues and questions that most interest you.

JWsurvey.org will need to be mentioned, if only because it was founded by yours truly back in 2011 with the help of my friend John Hoyle! Our aim was to make it possible for both current and former Witnesses to anonymously express their views in such a way that the results could be collated and analyzed. From a simple survey website, it soon grew into a blog/news website reporting on current developments in the Witness world. Over the years, JWsurvey has become one of the most popular online resources for ex-Witnesses, typically attracting around 100,000 visits per month. At the time of writing, we have a small editorial team committed to covering various important news stories involving Watchtower as they arise.

WatchtowerDocuments.org is Barbara Anderson's invaluable archive of Watchtower materials stretching back to the Russell era, including early publications and official correspondence. A former Bethelite in Watchtower's writing department, Barbara was uniquely positioned to witness the organization's indifference when concerns about child sex abuse first surfaced in the 1980's and 1990's. Barbara is now a prominent and much-loved ex-Witness activist, and her online biography (look for the page "Discoveries of Barbara Anderson") is a must-read.

Quotes-Watchtower.co.uk is a dated but nicely organized website offering a series of remarkable quotes, listed alphabetically according to subject. If you ever find yourself wavering over whether Watchtower might, at some point, have been a conduit of divine wisdom, be sure to browse this wonderful collection of outrageous snippets from early Watchtower literature. You will find that it superbly lays bare the self-indulgence and eccentricity of the "faithful slave" over many decades.

The above websites are certainly not the only ones exiting Witnesses will find useful but, along with AvoidJW.org, I consider them the most effective online resources if you need quick access to information debunking Watchtower dogma and you are not in a position to fill your bookshelf with "apostate" books that—quite apart from leaving you with an eye-watering Amazon bill—may get you in trouble with believing friends and family members.

There are other websites, including forums and social media pages, that do an excellent job of bringing ex-Witnesses together to debrief each other and share information. I will mention some of these in a later chapter. Suffice to say, the internet is brimming with superbly-reasoned material about Jehovah's Witnesses if you know where to look.

Ex-Witness YouTube Channels

JWfacts is Paul Grundy's YouTube presence, featuring a number of excellent videos showcasing his trademark logic and calm, non-sensationalist reasoning. His video titled *Growing up a Jehovah's Witness 1960-2010* is thoughtfully made and explores the impact of Watchtower's stigmatization of higher education on multiple generations of Witnesses.

John Cedars is my own channel (I could hardly write this list without at least some mention!) on which I offer rebuttals to Watchtower videos and interview individuals who have joined me in leaving Watchtower and other harmful belief systems. I have also released a number of videos addressing specific topics relevant to Jehovah's Witnesses such as the United Nations NGO scandal, the 607 B.C.E. teaching, and Watchtower's mishandling of child abuse.

Though I am more open about my atheism on my YouTube videos—especially when it comes to refuting Watchtower's anti-evolution rhetoric—I like to think my viewers understand that my opinions are offered on a take-it-or-leave-it basis. I certainly do not expect all who watch my videos to agree with me on everything or join me in abandoning religion altogether.

askreality is a channel by an ex-Mormon named Chris. There are only a small number of videos (eight at the time of writing), but each of them are superbly crafted to tell different stages of Chris' journey of awakening from his Mormon indoctrination.

Comparing different high control groups is an excellent means of gauging whether you have been caught up in one. In this case, by examining the claims of Jehovah's Witnesses, Chris learned valuable lessons about the nature of faith that proved extremely helpful in discarding his own deeply-engrained religious assumptions.

ApostateChick produces excellent vlog-style videos in which she gives her perspective on various Witness-related issues and dilemmas, often with a welcome injection of humor and wit (and even the occasional bit of rapping)!

Telltale Atheist takes a broader look at cults and atheism in general, but he will often focus on his experiences with the Witness faith. Telltale's trademark style of narrating while an illustration unfurls on the screen is very relaxing, and the information is well organized and presented.

Ex-JW Fifth is the channel of a former Bethelite, pioneer and ministerial servant going by the name of "Fifth" who has recorded a series of insightful interviews with individuals who have similarly forged a path to mental freedom.

ExGileadMissionary was a YouTuber who put out a small number of videos between 2008 and 2010 before going silent. His videos are extremely well-informed due to the fact that their maker went through Watchtower's Gilead training program (as the channel name suggests!) and was helped to awaken partly due to being underwhelmed by the "spiritual food" on offer. The relaxed, instructional style of the videos, together with the skillful use of the Bible, make them extremely relatable for those only just finding their way out of Witness indoctrination.

There are many more YouTubers I could mention, such as **Danmera, CandleSurgeon, Kameron Fader** and **Susan Gaskin** to name just a few. The beauty of YouTube is that anyone can make their voice heard simply by getting in front of the camera and sharing their experience—something that you may be able to do some day if you feel so inclined, or as your circumstances allow.

For those in a position to "out" themselves in this way, there are few more effective ways to raise awareness before hundreds or even thousands of people than with a heartfelt, compelling personal testimony. Very often the videos with the least production and editing, where the subject is candidly opening up on camera without any pretensions or expectations, garner the highest number of views.

REGRESSIVE EX-WITNESS YOUTUBE VIDEOS

Of course, while a good number of YouTube videos are extremely helpful in showing Witness viewers the other side of the argument, some ex-Witness YouTubers allow their hatred of Watchtower, and even other ex-Witnesses, to obscure their message. Rather than simply telling their story or conveying helpful information, they descend into rants, character assassinations, and stirring up controversy. Sadly, this small but vocal minority of ex-Witness YouTubers advocate harassment and intimidation of bewildered Witnesses in public or at their places of worship, or indulge in lengthy diatribes against other ex-Witnesses of whom they disapprove.

Of course, it could be that you find material like this entertaining. Everyone has their own tastes, and the highest trending videos on YouTube are not always the most edifying! Sometimes it can be fascinating to watch someone losing it on camera. It is also important to acknowledge that there is a role for healthy debate and disagreement in any community. If ex-Witnesses only ever patted each other on the back and agreed on everything, something would be very wrong! As ugly and unsettling as infighting and bickering can be at times, it is also an encouraging indicator that the ex-Witness movement is growing and more diverse voices are being added. As more Witnesses escape and involve themselves in activism, bringing with them differing attitudes and ideas, friction will be inevitable.

With all that said, it is important that you do not let the ugly side of YouTube apostasy dishearten you, or cause you to abort your escape. Not every voice in the growing melting pot of ex-Witness YouTube videos will be one of kindness, logic and reason, and it is worth bearing this in mind when you are first finding your feet. If you stumble on videos of ex-Witnesses behaving in a way that is far from mature, calm and level-headed, please do not assume all ex-Witnesses are like this. It is simply a case of many different individuals finding their own paths out of the movement. Not every journey has brought the person to a place in their life where they can harness their justified anger in a healthy way.

In conclusion, there are any number of resources upon which you can draw to aid you in reaching a clear understanding of precisely how you have been deceived, and to what extent. They can be found digitally or in hard copy, in text form or videos, and you do not need to necessarily spend any money to access quality information that will help you figure things out.[10] Though it may be easier and less distressing to forgo research and simply satisfy yourself that you have made the correct decision ("It's a cult—I just know it and I don't need any books or website to tell me that!") I would urge that a more studious, investigative approach will reap dividends in the long run.

The human mind is a breathtakingly complex thing—so complex that doubts and fears can linger long after you have satisfied yourself that there is no monster under the bed. As I have already explained in the previous chapter, you will be far better equipped to purge these residual dark thoughts if your mind has a repository of reassuring, factual information to call upon whenever deeply-ingrained paranoias and insecurities surface.

---

[10] Even books that would be costly to purchase can be accessed for free if you loan them from your local library. Most libraries are unlikely to have an extensive selection of ex-Witness literature, but they will normally allow you to order a title that you are interested in reading.

Doing research, however, is just one piece of the puzzle when you are first coming to terms with the nauseating realization that years or even decades of your life have been swallowed up in service to one of many cult-like groups. Of equally pressing importance is the need to extricate yourself from Watchtower's tendrils with as little damage as possible, especially when it comes to cherished relationships with family and friends. For this, you will need an exit plan.

CHAPTER THREE

PLANNING YOUR EXIT

THERE are two ways to escape Jehovah's Witnesses. You can do so formally by disassociating, or informally by becoming inactive—otherwise known as "fading." The difference between the two could be likened to leaving an excruciatingly dull party by simply putting on your coat and walking out the door long before the party is over, thus incurring the wrath of your host and fellow guests, or excusing yourself in a less obvious way.

Rather than announcing that you are leaving because you are not enjoying yourself, you might apologetically tell your host that you are urgently needed back home and you will be returning later if you have time. Your host and the other guests spend the rest of the evening assuming you will be rejoining them, gradually getting so drunk they hardly notice your absence. Both strategies will get you out of the door, but the impact on those you are leaving behind differs significantly.

It could be that you have no reason to care what your host or fellow party-goers think of you. Perhaps you barely know them and it would be no huge deal if they think you are the biggest jerk ever. But if your relationship with these people is important to you—perhaps they are your workmates and you wish to avoid needless acrimony in the workplace—you will want to manage their feelings to the extent possible even if doing so requires an element of deception. In the case of these people being your workmates, you have more to lose by your job being made difficult than they have to lose by being duped into thinking you might be returning.

This is roughly the dilemma you face when deciding whether to fade or disassociate. The decision you make will largely depend on the extent to which you rely on personal relationships with those still mentally trapped inside the organization—especially if they are close family members.

Of course, it should be the case that your personal, conscientious choice to leave will be respected and everyone will react to your decision like adults, maintaining their friendship with you irrespective of whether you continue to share their beliefs. Since 1981, however, Jehovah's Witnesses have been an organization from which it is impossible to leave with dignity. From the moment the following words were printed in the September 15, 1981, *Watchtower,* disassociation has been punishable by shunning:

> Persons who make themselves "not of our sort" by deliberately rejecting the faith and beliefs of Jehovah's Witnesses should appropriately be viewed and treated as those who have been disfellowshiped for wrongdoing.

If you face the dilemma of whether to fade or disassociate, perhaps because you have loved ones still inside, you might read the above and consider your choice to be an obvious one. You might think of fading as the perfect loophole to exploit, allowing you to escape with family relationships continuing as normal. But this is not always the case.

GOING INACTIVE

Once your absence from meetings and ministry becomes noticeable, you may be deemed "bad association" and subjected to a degree of shunning even though you are still technically a Witness. I call this "preemptive shunning," because you are receiving punishment in anticipation of what you have not yet done, i.e. leaving the faith altogether. But unlike those who disassociate, inactive ones are afforded a measure of sympathy and goodwill by the organization. For example, in 2015 a brochure was released, titled *Return to Jehovah*, designed to reach out to such ones. As you would expect, the writers demonstrated that they are incapable of envisioning any circumstance under which a Witness might fade that does not involve the individual being somehow at fault.—See box "A Brief Guide to the Brochure *Return to Jehovah*."

Though there may be goodwill and patience extended to faders, it is conditional on a number of factors, namely (1) whether they continue to believe, (2) how long they remain inactive, and (3) whether they uphold Watchtower's standards.

As I will discuss in more detail in the next chapter, elders will usually not hesitate to take action if they come to learn that an inactive one is actually an unbeliever—especially if that one is open about their apostasy.

When it comes to the length of inactivity, Witnesses are encouraged to think of you as bloodguilty if you continue to neglect involvement in the preaching work. For example, in a talk given at a branch visit to Trinidad in January 2018, Governing Body member Anthony Morris read Ezekiel 33:8, 9. ("I will ask [the blood of the wicked man] back from you.") Morris then asked all in attendance (including those tied in over video link) to look at their hands, before saying:

> Only God, as he looks at your hands in here and all those that are tied in. . . does he see blood there?

A BRIEF GUIDE TO THE BROCHURE
Return to Jehovah

Return to Jehovah

As you begin to distance yourself from the organization, you might find yourself being offered the *Return to Jehovah* brochure by elders or believing friends and relatives. Published in 2015, the brochure is apparently an effort by Watchtower to counter the impact of Witnesses leaving by encouraging inactive ones to return.

The writers of the brochure rely on the reader being emotionally tied to the organization, perhaps as a result of never having done objective research into their beliefs (which is no doubt the case with many who fall into being inactive). No consideration is given to the possibility that the inactive one may have made a conscientious decision to leave as a result of the abusive elements of Watchtower teachings, or has come to the conclusion that Witness theology is not objectively true.

For example, Part One of the brochure suggests that inactive ones are "lost sheep" who are "bewildered" and in need of Jehovah's protection. If they will only "recall [their] experiences as [they] came to know Jehovah" they will surely return.

Part Two explores anxiety as a reason for inactivity, perhaps due to "financial troubles, family problems, or health concerns." "Jehovah is understanding," the reader is assured. "He never expects more from us than we can give."

Part Three asks the reader whether they are holding a grudge, with "hurt feelings" lingering over the actions of other Witnesses in the congregation. "Our heavenly Father is aware of everything," the brochure insists, alluding to the assumption—common among Witnesses—that all wrongs within the organization will magically right themselves in time. The reader is reminded that "when we let go of resentment, we benefit ourselves."

Part Four asks whether the reader is avoiding the organization due to guilt. "Jehovah does not want you to keep suffering with a guilty conscience," they are told. "Today, Jehovah has provided congregation elders who have been trained to help repentant sinners restore their relationship with Jehovah." In this scenario, the inactive one is assumed to be at fault for some sin they might be concealing. And, of course, the strong likelihood of them returning only to be disfellowshipped and estranged from their family is glossed over.

Part Five summarizes by asking the reader to return to "the Shepherd and Overseer of Your Souls." "Returning to Jehovah is absolutely the best thing you can do," the writers insist. "Why? You will bring joy to Jehovah's heart. . . . Really, nothing can compare to the happiness we experience from giving Jehovah the worship he deserves."

A final opportunity to address the possibility of the reader simply no longer believing, or being appalled by the organization's lies and abuses, is missed. Instead, readers are beckoned to the nearest Kingdom Hall. "You can be sure that members of the congregation will warmly welcome you," says the brochure. "Rather than criticize or judge you, they will confirm their love for you and do whatever they can to encourage you."

But judgment is exactly what awaits a Witness who can no longer bring themselves to believe, and whose unbelief becomes known to elders. The "love" that awaits the returning inactive one is entirely conditional on them sharing the same devotion and unquestioning allegiance to the every word and whim of a New York-based hierarchy that will not hesitate to crush any dissent.

If you receive this brochure as a fader, it might be best to keep any reply to a minimum, or avoid sending a reply altogether—especially if there is a possibility of the recipient passing your message on to the elders. If a reply is necessary, you might say: "I appreciate the thoughtful gesture. I will let you know if I decide to act on any of the suggestions. In the meantime, please be assured of my love and best wishes."

My own believing friends and family know better than to send me this brochure. But, in the unlikely event of one appearing in my mail, as a disassociated Witness and known apostate my reply would be as follows:

"Thank you for caring enough about me to send this material. Please understand that what matters most to me is whether the religion is true or not. If you share my concern for truth, please explain to me how it can be objectively proven that Jehovah's Witnesses are exclusively God's organization. Once I receive compelling evidence along these lines, I will follow the advice on page 14 and attend my nearest meeting as soon as possible. Until then, please be assured that I am not lost, anxious or guilt-ridden, and I am not consumed by a craving to return to anything or anyone. I am happy now that I am living an authentic life in which I am free to pursue intellectual honesty and be loved for who I am rather than who others require me to be. If I don't hear from you again, I wish you every happiness no matter how you decide to live your life. If you are ever in need of my help for any reason, or if you just want to have a chat without discussing religion, I want you to know I am here for you."

Humans sitting next to you, they might have an idea because they know you well and you haven't been out in service in weeks. Well, guess what? Most likely God's seeing some blood all over your hands. Or they go totally inactive—and we appeal to them, we try to help—but you cannot water down what God says here. If your hands are not clean because you've been out warning, then they have blood on 'em and you're gonna lose your life!

Granted, the "faithful slave" are rarely this blunt in their publications. Nonetheless, the above words well represent their view of those who fail to preach their ideas, and it is a view that filters down to ordinary Witnesses. If you neglect to warn people that they will die at Armageddon unless they become Jehovah's Witnesses, in their eyes you become worthy of death yourself.

Then there is the challenge of remaining blameless as regards wrongdoing of any sort. For example, consider the following words that were included in the outline for a talk titled "Shun Unrepentant Wrongdoers" at the 2016 "Remain Loyal to Jehovah" convention:

Loyal Christians would not associate with "anyone called a brother" who is practicing serious sin[.] This is true even if no congregation action has been taken, as may be the case with an inactive one (*w85* 7/15 19 ¶14)

Hence, Witnesses are urged to shun inactive ones if it becomes known that they are involved in "serious sin" even if there has been no action taken by the elders. This means that, in addition to ensuring that nobody comes to learn of your apostasy, you also need to be perceived as sticking to Watchtower's standards in the minds of any believing friends or relatives with whom you are in contact. This may seem achievable to begin with, but as time drags on you may find maintaining a "whiter than white" image to be extremely problematic.

For example, perhaps you are a young, unmarried Witness who stops believing and decides to fade. In time, you might get involved with someone sexually whom you love deeply, but to whom you are not yet married. Your partner might want to meet your believing Witness parents, and feel hurt when you tell him or her that this would not be a good idea—or that they can only meet your parents if nothing is said that might raise suspicion that there is a sexual side to your relationship.

Over time, this kind of subterfuge and lack of transparency could place a considerable strain on your relationship, or on any future relationships. After all, you cannot expect those not raised as Witnesses to fully understand what is at stake, or to participate in a cover-up of something that is perfectly natural. Your partner may feel, with some justification, that life is too short to become embroiled in a relationship where they are made to feel like a naughty child just for having sex before marriage.

Unmarried escapees from Watchtower are not the only ones who may struggle to maintain a semblance of purity as far as the organization is concerned. While I was preparing this book, I interviewed ex-Witness Jill Long for my YouTube channel and heard her story of being disfellowshipped, along with her husband, because Witnesses in her neighborhood had spotted the Christmas lights adorning her front porch.[1]

Jill and her husband were not vocal opposers and had not been causing the congregation any trouble, but their elders still saw fit to hunt them down and disfellowship them five years after they had attended their last meeting simply because they were visibly celebrating a holiday of which the religion disapproves.

Interestingly, this exact scenario—of a faded Witness being disfellowshipped for outwardly celebrating Christmas—was brought up by Senior Counsel Angus Stewart when he questioned Governing Body member Geoffrey Jackson as part of Australia's Royal Commission into Institutional Responses to Child Sexual Abuse.[2] Their brief exchange on this issue provides a stunning example of the organization's dishonesty in instances where Watchtower officials are publicly cornered on the more shameful aspects of the faith:

> STEWART: So, for example, if they had become inactive or sought to fade without formally disassociating, and the elders came to visit and found them celebrating Christmas or a birthday, they would be found to be in transgression of the rules, would they not?

> JACKSON: That is not my understanding. But again, as I said, it is not my field, that goes into policy with regard

---

[1] The interview features in episode one of a series of videos on my channel titled *Fade, Interrupted: When the Elders Come Calling*.

[2] The issue of fading was brought up to highlight the fact that there is no easy way for Witnesses to leave and move on with their lives, which is especially problematic for victims of sexual molestation whose abuse has been mishandled by elders. Such ones who wish to fade could, in the scenario given, find themselves further victimized by an organization already responsible for exacerbating their suffering.

to those type of things, but from my personal experience, that's not the case.

Despite pleading ignorance, Jackson was knowingly lying when giving this testimony, as Jill's experience vividly demonstrates. Apart from being a Governing Body member, and therefore directly answerable for the disfellowshipping policy and its various connotations, Jackson is also an elder and therefore familiar with the contents of the *"Shepherd the Flock of God"* manual, which on page 65 includes "celebrating false religious holidays" among the criteria for apostasy—an offense warranting judicial action.

Hence, even though fading may seem the obvious choice as your preferred escape route, depending on your circumstances you would be well advised to not assume it will all be plain sailing. In the eyes of Watchtower, once you are baptized you must remain accountable to their rules and teachings *for life!* Years may pass after you have walked out of the Kingdom Hall for the last time, but it is still possible for you to be hunted down and punished by elders who insist on holding you to your baptismal vows, as countless ex-Witnesses like Jill will attest.[3]

FACING THE DILEMMA

With so much hanging in the balance, it must be acknowledged that nobody can make the decision on *how* to escape but you, since it is you who must live with the consequenc-

---

[3] You might be thinking that moving far away from those who think of you as a Witness would be a protection against judicial action for breaking the rules in some way, but even with this strategy there are no guarantees. In the same video in which Jill is interviewed, I also hear the story of ex-Witness Vincent Deporter. Vincent lives in Arizona and was tracked down by elders in France, his country of origin, when they learned of his apostasy.

es. Don't ever let anyone accuse you of cowardice or deception if you choose to fade rather than disassociate. After all, it is Watchtower that is trampling your human rights by putting you in this position and it is your right to make the best of a bad situation, using whatever means are at your disposal to preserve relationships that are important to you where possible.

This is not some test of bravery where you get a ticker-tape parade for going out with a bang and showing Watchtower who is boss. There is a lot to be said for fading being the preferable option if you are in a position to pursue that course, even if there are no guarantees that life as an inactive Witness will be trouble-free.

Conversely, if you decide to disassociate, no Witness friends or family should make you feel bad for making a conscientious stand for what you believe in. Of course, this may not stop them from making sniping remarks designed to make you feel guilty, ("You have betrayed Jehovah and his organization! You could have gone inactive but instead you are pursuing a prideful course!") but these are wholly unjustified and amount to bullying and intimidation.

Watchtower is the aggressor in this case and most certainly not you! It is Watchtower that has orchestrated a situation in which everyone must recognize the "faithful slave's" leadership or face exile. By distancing yourself from beliefs you know to be false despite juvenile threats of family estrangement ("Believe what I believe, or I'm not going to talk to you!"), you are pursuing the same course of honesty and integrity that Watchtower requires of converts who join from other religions.

With all that said, there are definitely pros and cons to consider when it comes to disassociating versus fading, and these should be weighed carefully before you make a final decision. For simplicity, on the following pages I have compiled the table "Likelihood of Being Shunned—Fading vs. Disassociation" to help you compare the two scenarios.

Despite the gravity of the dilemma facing you if you are deciding whether to fade or disassociate, you will usually have time on your side for reaching a decision. Your goal should not be to achieve perfection in your family life, because if Watchtower is influencing your loved ones this will be impossible. Rather, try to reach a point where you can at least look back and say that you have no regrets as to how you dealt with matters. If you take as much time as possible to ponder your predicament and decide which course to take, usually you will be able to make an informed decision and plan your exit accordingly, confident that, whatever happens, you have done your best.

EXECUTING A FADE

If your decision is to fade, you need to think about how quickly or slowly you will execute your fade. A gradual fade will be less noticeable. You might devise a plan for easing off on meetings or ministry that looks something like this:

Beginning: 8 meetings and 10 hours per month
After 3 months: 6 meetings and 8 hours per month
After 6 months: 4 meetings and 5 hours per month
After 9 months: 2 meetings and 2 hours per month
After 12 months: 0 meetings and 0 hours per month

Of course, even with such a gradual withdrawal from the congregation, your fade may draw some attention from elders. If this happens, I have prepared some material in the next chapter to help you keep elders at arm's length.

It may also be worthwhile to consider fading by moving to another congregation, perhaps in another part of the country, to minimize the likelihood of awkward encounters with Witnesses who know you while you are out shopping. If you move to a new congregation, a new body of elders that is not accustomed to seeing you at the Kingdom Hall is far less likely to notice you steadily reducing the number of hours and meetings per month. You may even get away with a much more rapid fade over, say, a couple of months.

WAKING UP AS A YOUNG PERSON

If you are a young person still living with parents and you have awoken from Watchtower indoctrination, your exit plan will probably be much more complicated. You may need to think about the possibility of flying the nest as part of your escape.

Much will depend on how zealous for "the truth" your parents are, and how much they are pressuring you to conform to their beliefs. Honest conversations may be needed at some point to test the water and prepare your folks for what lies ahead. If they react badly and make it clear that living under their roof is conditional on attending the Kingdom Hall and going out in service week in, week out, it may be worth exploring what opportunities are available for pursuing your independence.

It could be that, in the face of inflexibility from your parents, there is no realistic prospect of moving out and finding your own place in the foreseeable future. If this is the case, there is no shame in "faking it" until circumstances finally align in your favor. You never asked to be railroaded from infancy into following your parents' reli-

LIKELIHOOD OF BEING SHUNNED—FADING VS. DISASSOCIATION

	Fading	Disassociation
Shunning by believing workmates	Possible. Much will depend on the individual and how much interaction they need to have with you on a daily basis. You might notice no difference, but if they come to think of you as just as "worldly" as everyone else, expect conversations to become increasingly strained.	Likely. Sometimes workmates will be able to reason that they can interact with you so long as things are kept strictly professional. Others may feel that they need to change their employment (or fire you, if they are your superior!) to avoid risk of being spiritually contaminated by frequent contact with an avowed unbeliever.
Shunning by believing friends	Likely. Even though you are not officially disassociated, you will still be deemed "bad association" for failing to attend meetings. Much will depend on the individual. Close friends will not be reprimanded for spending time with you unless you develop a reputation as an apostate.	Inevitable. Your friends could face judicial action if they fail to shun you.

	Fading	Disassociation
Shunning by believing family	Possible. Your family may interpret your failure to attend meetings as evidence that you are spiritually weak and scale back on the amount of time they spend with you, but they are not required to completely shun you.	Highly likely. In some cases, family relationships can be maintained, such as between a disassociated father and his young believing son or daughter. But if you are not living under the same roof, or you are a son or daughter who is old enough to fend for themselves, expect to be completely cut off.
Shunning by a believing spouse	Unlikely. As difficult as it will be for your spouse to accept your inactivity, in reality there is scope for a wide variety of circumstances among married couples in any given congregation, including couples where the husband or wife has drifted but his or her spouse still attends meetings.	Possible. Though apostasy is not grounds for divorce, "absolute endangerment of spiritual life" is grounds for separation, which will in turn lead to shunning and, as the marriage deteriorates, divorce may become inevitable. Much will depend on whether your elders put pressure on your husband or wife to separate, and how willing he or she is to follow that advice.

gion and you cannot be blamed for making the best of a bad situation.

Walk the walk and talk the talk for as long as is needed, all the while doing everything you can to advance your education and prepare for independence, whether by investigating the state funding options for university or searching for a well-paying part-time job that will allow you to save money. With time and persistence, the day will inevitably come when you can drop the pretense, pack your bags, and start out by yourself.

Though your parents may be unsupportive or even hostile when you finally seize your opportunity to flee, try not to be too distraught or take things too personally. There is always the chance that, as you continue to show them love and kindness, they will soften their stance or even begin to sympathize with your reasons for leaving.

Whatever happens, even if your parents outright shun you, try to stay positive! If you are breaking free from the organization at a young age, you have much to be thankful for. There are many ex-Witnesses who would give a great deal to have escaped while they were still young, with their lives ahead of them, rather than wasting decades in service to Watchtower.

THE THREAT OF SHUNNING

Whatever your circumstances, as sad as it may be, it would be worthwhile to brace yourself for a worst case scenario in which your fade does not succeed and you end up shunned as an apostate despite your best efforts to keep everyone happy.

Try to prepare yourself emotionally for this possibility by remembering that your loved ones are not in full possession of their minds. If you begin to sense they are withdrawing from you, try not to lash out angrily, or say anything that will confirm Watchtower's stereotype of resentful, bitter apostates.

Of course, this can be easier said than done. I personally reacted with a great deal of anger when my father confirmed he would be shunning me. But, as they say, time is a healer. In the years that followed since that encounter, I have found that simple acts of love and kindness are far more productive, if only because they make me feel less guilt about my behavior.

I am often reminded of carers for Alzheimer's patients, and the way they will play along with the delusions of their clients because contradicting them, or trying to pull them back into reality, would be too distressing. Once you fully understand what you are up against, and accept that unloving words and actions on the part of those shunning you are the result of Watchtower pulling the strings, this will help you react with less frustration and more empathy. Over time, you may find the situation becomes more tolerable even if it is far from perfect.

In addition to preparing yourself emotionally, it may also be prudent to take practical measures to hold on to treasured memories while you are still in the good graces of your believing family. Are there any precious heirlooms that you can ask to take with you, or cherished photographs that you can scan digitally?

If you anticipate a worst case scenario of your fade collapsing into total shunning, you can use the time now to prepare fully rather than look back with regret later on. It may be that you are not the sentimental type and have no interest in photos and trinkets, but there is certainly nothing wrong with holding on to pleasant memories of good times spent with friends and family, even if these were predicated on you all being believers. Regardless of the circumstances, these are as much your memories as they are theirs.

IF YOU DECIDE TO DISASSOCIATE

It could be that, having considered all of the above, you decide against fading. You resolve instead that your exit plan must involve a clean break with the organization by disassociating (either now or at some future point) regardless of any concerns over shunning.

If this is the case, I have included a few sample disassociation letters from which you can choose. Please bear in mind that these are only intended as suggestions! It may be that you relish the prospect of writing to your elders in your own words. Even so, you might find the following templates helpful.

Template 1: This is as short and to-the-point as it gets. If you simply want to disassociate and wash your hands of the organization as expediently as possible, you might send the following message to your elders:

To whom it may concern,

Henceforth, let it be known that I, [insert name], do not wish to be associated in any way with Jehovah's Witnesses.

Sincerely,

[signed]

Template 2: If you feel the urge to use your letter of disassociation to reach out to your elders and maybe leave them with something to ponder, you can say the following:

Dear brothers

I regret to inform you that with immediate effect I am disassociating as one of Jehovah's Witnesses.

I have reached this decision after much careful thought and appreciate you respecting it. There will be no need for you to visit me for confirmation.

I understand that you may feel sadness that I am leaving the congregation, but this is something I feel I must do as a matter of conscience. I can no longer affiliate myself with an organization that has a growing reputation for failing to protect children and covering up child sex abuse. I am also no longer convinced that the Governing Body can claim to be sole custodians of divine truth, to the point of breaking up families through shunning if their teachings are contradicted.

Please understand that I am very fond of you all and will consider you as friends even if you decide to shun me. If you individually decide to pay me a visit, you will be received with warmth and love, and any conversations we have will remain strictly between us.

With love

[signed]

Template 3: If you have believing family, clients or workmates, and you wish to threaten legal action in the event of them being manipulated to shun you by elders, you can try a more forthright approach:

To whom it may concern

Henceforth, let it be known that I, [insert name], do not wish to be associated in any way with Jehovah's Witnesses.

Please be advised that I will vigorously defend my rights to freedom of conscience, to the extent of responding with legal action under [local/state] law if I suffer damages to my [family relationships/employment/business] as a consequence of my decision to disassociate.

Sincerely,

[signed]

Now that we have weighed the pros and cons of fading and disassociating, and explored what is involved in planning your exit, we can spend some time preparing you for various other practical issues you may face. In the next chapter, I will give you a heads up on what to expect from your elders as you progress with your escape.

CHAPTER FOUR

ELDERS ARE NOT ON YOUR SIDE

A BELIEVING Jehovah's Witness would find the title of this chapter alarming and almost impossible to grasp. They would see it as an affront to the brothers who, they may feel, selflessly and lovingly preside over them. Elders are considered spiritual shepherds whose primary focus is to minister to the needs of the flock. They are "gifts in men" provided by Jehovah for the "building up of the congregation." Why would they not be on your side?

Consider what is said on page 30 of *Organized to Do Jehovah's Will*. After listing the benefits of the elder arrangement, the book says:

> Their efforts to protect the flock from harmful elements, such as wicked men, contribute to our security.

In other words, a key responsibility of elders is that of protecting the congregation from anything deemed by Watchtower to be a "harmful element." Anyone who is considered "wicked," including those who have turned their backs on "Jehovah's organization," will be identified as a threat and dealt with accordingly.

You may be reading this as an aspiring ex-Witness with many friends who are elders, some of whom may be kind, sincere men. Despite accepting that they are loyal to Watchtower, you may find it impossible to imagine them turning on you. "Bill is such a sweet guy," you could reason.

"I'm sure if I have him over for a coffee and explain my doubts, he will understand. He may even agree with some of my reasons for distancing myself from the organization."

If this describes your feelings, allow me to tell you a story that will hopefully put things in perspective. You see, I was once "Bill"—your friendly neighborhood elder who could be confided in regarding almost anything without freaking out. I took my duties as a spiritual shepherd very seriously and tried to be a good listener when members of the congregation approached me with problems. Because I had doubts myself (albeit very well suppressed doubts) I would have been sympathetic to someone who was struggling with their beliefs. But my loyalty was, above all else, to the "faithful slave."

Soon after being appointed as an elder, I was briefed about a situation where a recently-divorced sister who had moved into the congregation had become romantically involved with a local brother before her divorce was final. The sister's "fleshly" (or actual) brother was also the coordinator of the body of elders, and he was apparently fixated on retribution, having warned her not to get romantically involved so soon after the collapse of her marriage. He decided that his sister, who we will call "Ruth," needed to be disciplined by being "marked" together with her boyfriend.

Marking is a form of soft shunning where the congregation must refrain from social activities with a person who is identified in a special talk by their conduct rather than by name. This punitive measure—intended for behavior that is "disorderly" but does not constitute gross sin—is supposed to end once the reason for the marking no longer exists and the elders take the lead in socializing with the marked person again.

I had grave concerns about the whole situation. I strongly suspected that the elder body was being manipulated into taking sides in what was essentially a family dispute. Nevertheless, my calls for leniency fell mostly on deaf ears and it was decided that, even though the divorce papers had finally come through (hence the reason for the marking no longer existed), Ruth and her partner must be cut off from socializing with the congregation.[1] As an elder, it was my responsibility to go along with what the rest of the elder body had decided and uphold the decision even though it made no sense to me personally.

I will never forget being tasked, along with another elder, to sit down with a ministerial servant who was known to be having difficulties accepting the elder body's decision. This ministerial servant was a close friend of the couple and had made it known that he disagreed with the way they were being treated. It was my job, and the job of the other elder, to make it clear that he was to show support for what had been decided regardless of his personal feelings, because otherwise his qualifications as a servant could be called into question. In other words, the message was: "fall in line, or be demoted."

I saw the encounter as an opportunity to demonstrate to my fellow elders that, though somewhat of a young rookie, I could be relied on to attend to difficult matters. I therefore did the majority of the talking while my fellow

---

[1] Eventually, a letter would be received from the London branch advising the body that the marking should have ended once the divorce papers came through. Unfortunately, by the time this letter was received and the advice implemented, considerable damage had been done in the congregation with no punitive action taken against the coordinator for using the body to serve his personal agenda.

elder mostly sat back and watched. The ministerial servant was understandably bewildered and frustrated, but ultimately yielded—much to my relief (because I liked him and felt it would be a huge waste for the congregation to lose his services).

Today, I look back and shudder that I could be capable of such thuggish behavior, despite the consolation of knowing that I was not, at that time, in full possession of my own mind. Though I am relieved that, by happy coincidence, the twelve months that I spent as an elder before eventually standing down did not involve presiding in any judicial committees or disfellowshipping anyone, I am deeply ashamed that I was able to discard my principles and convictions so readily. But this is precisely what elders must be prepared to do if necessary.

An elder is effectively a line manager for Watchtower. He is not entitled to an opinion if this differs from that of the organization or the rest of the elder body. An elder's loyalty is, first and foremost, to the "faithful slave."

If an elder learns that a brother or sister in his congregation is having doubts—even if it is a close personal friend—their overriding concern is firstly to salvage the person by restoring their spirituality and urging them to "wait on Jehovah" (which amounts to suppressing their doubts). Failing that, an elder will not hesitate to protect the spirituality of the congregation by pursuing a course that will result in the avowed unbeliever being jettisoned as a "mentally diseased" apostate.

As pleasant, easy-going and amiable as an individual elder may be, ultimately he is bound by the same rules as all other elders and there can never be any exceptions. With this in mind, consider one of the criteria in a bulleted list about apostasy in the *"Shepherd the Flock of God"* manual, which governs the actions of all elders (bold and italics as in the original):

> **Deliberately spreading teachings contrary to Bible truth as taught by Jehovah's Witnesses:** (Acts 21:21, ftn.; 2 John 7, 9, 10) Any with sincere doubts should be helped. Firm, loving counsel should be given. (2 Tim. 2:16-19, 23-26; Jude 22, 23) If one obstinately *is speaking about or deliberately spreading false teachings,* this may be or may lead to apostasy. If there is no response after a first and a second admonition, a judicial committee should be formed.—Titus 3:10, 11; *w89* 10/1 p. 19; *w86* 4/1 pp. 30-31; *w86* 3/15 p. 15.

Consider, too, what is said about disassociation in the same publication:

> Whereas disfellowshipping is an action taken by a judicial committee against an unrepentant wrongdoer, disassociation is an action taken by an individual who no longer desires to be one of Jehovah's Witnesses. (1 John 2:19) The body of elders should appoint a committee of three elders to consider the facts.

In further defining disassociation, the *Shepherd* book presents another bulleted list of criteria which includes "joining another religious organization," "willingly and unrepentantly taking blood" (not being sorry about saving your life by taking blood is apparently a sin!) and "taking a course contrary to the neutral position of the Christian congregation" (i.e. pursuing a career in politics or gaining employment with a political organization). The first item in this list reads as follows (bold as in the original):

> **Making known a firm decision to be known no longer as one of Jehovah's Witnesses.** If the individual is agreeable, the committee should first try to speak with him and provide spiritual assistance. (Gal. 6:1) Does he

really desire to disassociate himself, or does he simply no longer want to associate actively with the congregation? Is the desire to disassociate prompted by doubts or discouragement? If he is adamant in his position, he should be encouraged to put his request in writing and sign it. If he does not, then the witnesses to his request should prepare a statement for the confidential files and sign it.

From the above material, all of which is to be consulted when elders are dealing with individuals who begin making the wrong noises about the organization, it should be clear that there is no room for flexibility when it comes to those who can no longer bring themselves to believe. If an elder visits you and hears you express doubts, you can soon find yourself in an extremely precarious situation unless you are willing to immediately backtrack, perhaps by saying that deep down you know it is the truth but you are simply feeling depressed or discouraged.

For as long as you can pay lip service to Watchtower's narrative of Witness teachings being absolute, unquestionable truth that a person will only struggle to embrace if he or she is spiritually sick, you stand a chance of coming through such an encounter relatively unscathed. But if an elder detects that you no longer want to be a Witness, or suspects that you are likely to spread apostate ideas to others, your predicament could rapidly deteriorate regardless of any past friendship.

Of course, it could be that, having given your unique circumstances careful thought and pondered some of the advice in the previous chapter about planning your exit, you are perfectly happy to disassociate from the Witnesses and you really do not care who knows it. It may be that you have no family who would shun you if you were to cut your ties with the Witnesses, or perhaps you do have family and loved ones but you have resolved that formally leaving the religion is the best for you irrespective of any shunning that ensues. If this is the case, then this chapter is mostly irrelevant to your predicament and you can move on to the next!

If, however, your exit plan involves fading and maintaining ties with believing family members despite no longer believing yourself, at least for the time being, you would be well advised to keep your elders at arm's length to the extent possible—even in the case of an elder who happens to be a good friend. You cannot underestimate the extent of his allegiance to Watchtower, or assume he would afford you special, preferential treatment if you were to reveal your doubts to him. The risks involved are simply too great.

It could be that an elder friend notices that you have been missing meetings and asks to call at your home for a coffee by himself. (Elders cannot pay such a visit if you are a woman at home alone. There would need to be two of them.) If there is only one elder involved, you are likely not yet under suspicion of apostasy. We can call this a yellow alert. In this situation, I would recommend making excuses and continually postponing the potential meeting until he gets the message and stops asking.

If a meeting becomes unavoidable, perhaps because he calls on you unannounced, I would advise keeping it as brief as possible. ("I hope you don't mind, but I need to dash out soon for an appointment.") Keep any personal information about yourself to an absolute minimum. If you are asked a direct question about your beliefs or spirituality, say something like: "I don't feel comfortable talking about that. I truly value you as a friend, but I have a lot going on right now and

I would rather approach you about my spirituality when it is right for me. I hope you can respect that."

If the elder persists despite this firm but polite snub, you are well within your rights to end the conversation. ("Don't take this the wrong way, but I've already told you how I feel and it seems as though you are not respecting my wishes. Thanks for dropping by, and I really appreciate the concern, but I have things I need to do today.")

If two elders try to arrange a visit, the same advice applies, namely to put off the visit for as long as possible until they give up. However, you should know that when two elders are involved, the situation is potentially more serious. We can call this an orange alert, wavering on red depending on the intentions.

Two elders means one of two things: (1) you are receiving a "shepherding visit," likely due to a period of inactivity, or (2) the two elders are really "two witnesses" and they are investigating you to determine whether a judicial committee needs to be formed.

In the case of a shepherding visit, the same conversational tips already given would apply if the elders call unannounced. As well-meaning as they might be, get them out of your door as expediently as possible and without them learning anything personal about you that they did not already know.

If you have somehow been forced into agreeing to a shepherding visit, perhaps by a relative in the same household, you should not feel bad about telling them precisely what they want to hear whether it is true or not. ("I do appreciate this visit. I have been feeling spiritually weak lately and it has caused me to miss some meetings. I'm sorry about that. It isn't always easy to get to the Kingdom Hall when you feel bad about not doing enough for Jehovah. If there are some scriptures you could share with me, I would like that.")

Though you have been taught to despise lying, and though lying is wrong, you need to understand that the wrong of misleading the elders on a personal matter that is really none of their business does not remotely compare with the wrong they can and will inflict on you if they learn the extent of your doubts. Shunning is a life-altering punishment that you are well-advised to avoid if at all possible until you are emotionally ready for it. You should feel no guilt about doing whatever is necessary to evade this grossly immoral and unbiblical penalty.[2]

Even if you were to feign mental or emotional problems, perhaps saying that you are currently seeing a therapist for severe depression (whether you are or not), any deception of this kind would be nothing compared to the brutality that is in store for you if your elders discover that you are embarking down a road of unbelief, or that you are doing something that could be deemed sinful. And because there are two of them, the requirement of two witnesses for judicial action over anything incriminating that is said will be satisfied according to official Watchtower procedure.

---

[2] While the Greek Scriptures do provide measures for preserving the spiritual cleanliness of a congregation by limiting social interaction with wrongdoers, none of these provisions insist on the break-up of families—especially to the point where family members are not to speak to one another. Jesus' parable of the prodigal son provides a powerful lesson that family ties come first above all else, because the father ran to welcome the son while he was "still a long way off"—in other words, regardless of whether repentance had been established. (Luke 15:20) As recently as 1947, even Watchtower publications concluded that excommunication is "altogether foreign to Bible teachings."—See January 8, 1947, *Awake!*

If two elders succeed in calling on you, and their intention is to pursue matters judicially, this should become apparent by the nature of their questioning. In a shepherding visit, the tone would be vague and positive: "We've really missed you at the hall lately and we thought it would be good to drop by and offer you some encouraging thoughts from the scriptures. Your spirituality is very important to us and we want to make sure you're getting all the help you need." In this case, the previous suggestions for handling the conversation apply. While appreciatively noting their concern, your objective should be to keep things brief and not divulge any information about you or your spirituality that they did not already know.

You will know that this is something other than a shepherding visit if the tone is the opposite of vague and positive, i.e. specific and negative: "A matter has come to our attention lately that has been a cause of great concern for us. We would like to establish exactly what has happened so that we can go about giving you spiritual assistance and ensuring the congregation is kept clean." In this case, I'm afraid the situation is infinitely more serious. You are being judicially investigated. We need to escalate to a red alert!

Navigating your way through any part of a judicial investigation is extremely stressful and problematic, and will largely depend on the nature of the investigation (is it for apostasy, or are they investigating you on some other grounds?) and, crucially, on the elders involved. Are they reasonable, liberal, empathetic elders, or are they heartless Watchtower goons who are frantically trying to uncover transgressions that they can penalize?

Assuming you want to remain as a Jehovah's Witness (albeit in name only) so that you can continue having family contact while figuring out your escape strategy, you will be well advised to do or say *anything* that will get you through the judicial process unscathed.

In my previous book, *The Reluctant Apostate,* I describe my own brush with elders when—while still a believer—I decided to involve them in personal indiscretions regarding my marriage. I wrote a letter detailing all the ways I had wronged my wife, and posted it through the front door of my coordinator.

A judicial committee resulted in which, despite the comprehensive details already divulged, I was interrogated in a needlessly invasive manner on extremely intimate matters. As I explain in my book, I now look back on the whole episode with nothing but regret and annoyance that I involved elders in deeply personal affairs that had nothing to do with them. I wrote that these men "had no more right to this information than my local postman or storekeeper."

The difference between your postman and an elder is that one has been deluded into believing he has been appointed by God's organization with the power to interfere in people's private lives under the pretext of rendering "spiritual assistance," while the other has not. In reality, neither are entitled to hear about your deeply personal affairs, whether these involve your sex life or your religious beliefs (or lack thereof). Any power that an elder has over you is therefore power you choose to give him! If an elder is little more than a line manager for an organization that has repeatedly proved throughout its history to be deceptive, blundering and harmful—ruthlessly prizing its own prosperity over the well-being of individuals to the extent of covering up child abuse on an unfathomable scale—then the elder should be granted no power whatsoever.

This is the mindset with which you must approach dealings with elders over judicial matters, but it is crucial that you do not let them realize that they no longer have power over you! If you are to keep your elders off your back, they need to assume that you respect their position and value their involvement even though you do not. Therefore, your tone should be respectful and accommodating. With this in mind, here are two scenarios that you might face, with suggestions on how to deflect accusations that may be leveled at you:

Scenario 1: A believing friend has told the elders that you have been "murmuring," or making disrespectful remarks about the organization.

Suggested response: "It's true that we had that conversation, but I don't remember expressing myself in quite that way. It sounds like so-and-so has misinterpreted something I've said, because quite frankly that is not the sort of thing I would say. I would need to think it in order to say it! I have certainly been struggling spiritually lately, but not to quite that extent. But I do appreciate so-and-so coming to speak to you about it so that I can put his/her mind at ease. I'm also grateful for the opportunity to have this conversation with you and get your help."

Scenario 2: A family member has discovered you reading or watching apostate material online and has informed the elders.

Suggested response: "I'm glad so-and-so has told you about this, because there has been a misunderstanding and I'm anxious to nip this in the bud. It's true that I have been struggling spiritually recently and I made the poor choice of seeing what apostates have to say so that I can test my ability to refute them. Of course, when I looked online I found the information very unsatisfying and not in harmony with what I have learned to be true from the faithful slave. But I can see how it would have looked to so-and-so, and I will apologize to him/her as soon as possible."

You might feel tempted to respond to the above two scenarios by being frank with the elders. You might be horrified at the thought of deceiving them and aspire to rescuing them from their indoctrination. You are perfectly entitled to try doing this, but you would be playing with fire by putting your cards on the table and being honest about your grievances. As likable as these men may be, and as much as you want to help them, what matters most in this situation is keeping your head off the chopping block so that you get to fight another day, whether by fading successfully or disassociating on your own terms and according to your own timescale.

If the two elders are unsatisfied with what you have told them, they will report back to the elder body and three elders will be selected to form a judicial committee. They will then inform you of a specific date and time for your judicial hearing—usually at the local Kingdom Hall. At this point, you have four options:

Option 1: Write a letter of disassociation. If your attempts at evasion have already failed to the point where a judicial committee has been convened, then your chances of making it through the judicial hearing itself are not promising. This might be the right time to accept your fate and save yourself the stress of being hauled before a kangaroo court in which three men get to play judge, jury and executioner—especially if attending would cause you great anxiety.

Yes, making a clean break with the organization is an ordeal in itself—an ordeal that I will try to walk you through with this book—but no matter how difficult your situation may be in the aftermath of disassociation, you can recover and lead a happy, fulfilled life as many others have done, myself included! You will find suggested letters of disassociation in the previous chapter.

Option 2: Attend the hearing with the objective of persuading the elders that you take Witness beliefs seriously and wish to cooperate with their efforts. To avoid disfellowshipping, you will need to display repentance regarding the accusations against you irrespective of whether they are true or not. If you deny the accusations, no matter how unjust they may be, the elders may feel they have little choice but to disfellowship you.

Because a judicial hearing has been convened, this means that your guilt has already been determined. All that remains, as far as the elders are concerned, is to establish your repentance. If you are deemed repentant, you will be reproved (meaning there may be an announcement and you will be restricted from commenting at meetings for a period). If you are deemed unrepentant, you will be disfellowshipped. There is therefore no point in pleading "not guilty," because—apart from this likely being interpreted as you trying to "minimize or justify [your] bad course"—if the elders were to drop the charges entirely this would require them to concede that there was no evidence for convening the judicial committee to begin with. And, like the organization they serve, elders are not renowned for admitting when they are wrong!

Before attending the meeting, it is important that you download a PDF copy of the *"Shepherd the Flock of God"* textbook, which can be easily found by a Google search. Carefully read pages 89 to 94 in the chapter titled "Judicial

Hearing Procedure."³ This will give you an invaluable insider look at what you can expect, allowing you to prepare your responses so that these conform as closely as possible to the elders' requirements for determining repentance. (For example, one of the "indications of repentance" is "contritely" praying to Jehovah and seeking "his forgiveness and mercy." Hence, without going overboard, you will want to tell the elders that you have repeatedly and fervently prayed for forgiveness.)

If you are sufficiently convincing, the elders will have no choice but to issue you with a reproof, meaning that you have avoided disfellowshipping and bought yourself some time to plan and execute your escape. If you are not convincing, or if the decision is made to disfellowship you no matter how convincing you are, then try not to lose heart. As soul-crushing as it can be to find yourself disfellowshipped, remember that this says nothing about you as a person and everything about how controlling, rule-obsessed and judgmental the organization is—an organization from which you are now free!

Option 3: Neglect to attend the meeting, in which case you could likely be disfellowshipped *in absentia*, with your absence interpreted as evidence that you do not want to cooperate with the judicial arrangement.

Option 4: Obtain a signed letter from a mental health professional or lawyer aimed at delaying judicial proceedings. If the elders receive a letter suggesting that you are under extreme stress and at risk of committing suicide if

³ Watchtower is continually updating its guidance to elders. If you are reading this book at a future point when a newer elder's manual is in circulation, hopefully you will still be able to locate a downloadable copy and consult the relevant pages on the judicial process.

they do not end their investigation, they may have no option but to delay or suspend the hearing. The same would be true if a letter is received threatening legal action, perhaps over the consequences to your family or employment if you are disfellowshipped and shunned.

Page 86 of the *Shepherd* manual makes the following provisions:

> In judicial cases where the accused threatens suicide, it may be best for the committee to suspend the hearing to focus on helping him regain his balance. . . . The judicial committee should communicate with the branch if there are questions about a certain case. . . . If the accused threatens legal action against the elders, the elders should suspend proceedings and promptly telephone the branch office.

Bear in mind that there are no guarantees that pursuing this fourth option will result in your escaping the attention of your elders. It could be that, after consulting with the branch office, the decision is made to pursue judicial action regardless—in which case you will have only succeeded in buying yourself a bit more time. In the case of legal action being threatened, acrimony and ill feeling will inevitably be stoked with your would-be inquisitors, potentially making an already volatile situation even worse. Even so, depending on your circumstances and how desperate you are to fend off judicial action, you may feel that extreme measures are warranted.

Of course, nobody but you can decide on which course to take. While the fears and concerns of close friends and family members who will be impacted by your decision deserve some consideration, ultimately this is your life. It is primarily you who will bear the brunt of the backlash if you make public your escape. Whatever path you choose, at least by carefully weighing your options you can have the satisfaction of knowing that you did your best under the circumstances.

Though it is appalling that Watchtower has put you in this position by making itself a captive organization, there is some consolation in knowing that, whatever happens, you are by no means alone in your struggle. When you visit Facebook groups and forums dedicated to ex-Jehovah's Witnesses, it soon becomes apparent that there are many who share your dilemma of pursuing conscientious freedom versus maintaining family ties.

Having personally faced this decision and chosen living an authentic life regardless of the impact on believing relatives, I can only say that I have no regrets—and my wife feels the same. If anything, we would have split with the organization sooner! As painful as the repercussions were in the immediate aftermath of disassociating, with many tears shed over the backlash from our Witness family, the joy and satisfaction we now feel for being true to who we are and living an authentic life far outweighs the difficulties we experienced during the initial firestorm. Escaping from Jehovah's Witnesses can be very much like a pregnancy. The pain can be excruciating and seemingly unending when you are in the moment, but the final result is so beautiful that it is all worthwhile in the end!

Now that you are fully briefed on what to expect from elders who may try to block your escape, we can now turn our attention to other areas in which caution is needed—including your use of the internet.

CHAPTER FIVE

PROTECT YOUR PRIVACY ONLINE

LIKELY you are already familiar with the need for a degree of caution when using the internet. You do not need me to tell you that opening the wrong kind of email can result in your computer getting infected with a virus or malware. You know that divulging too much personal information can result in hackers stealing your identity. But when you are in the process of escaping Jehovah's Witnesses, the internet carries an added danger: the threat of your apostasy being discovered by Witness friends and relatives, and judicial action being launched against you by elders before you are ready to formally break ties.

The trouble is that, despite these risks, the internet is also your lifeline. It is likely the source from which you have uncovered information debunking once cherished beliefs, thus starting you on the path to freedom. It is also a crucial resource for connecting with others in your situation and keeping up-to-date with ex-Witness meet-ups and events. So, how can you eliminate the risks of the internet while continuing to enjoy the benefits?

Of course, it could be that you do not mind whether you are discovered or not, because you are either disassociated or have resolved to disassociate soon. But if you are anxious to keep your apostasy below the radar for the time being, the following tips are worthy of your consideration when browsing online ex-Witness content.

Use a Pseudonym

Social media is a marvelous tool for keeping the world connected and allowing everyone to have a voice, but most social media platforms thrive on using your posts and comments to attract other members with little regard for your need for privacy.

Facebook in particular, though an extremely useful resource for bringing ex-Witnesses together, is geared toward broadcasting your every "like" or comment to everyone who knows you or stands a chance of knowing you, because the more Facebook users there are (and the more interconnected they are) the more profitable Facebook will be.

It is therefore crucial that you avoid "liking," sharing, or commenting on anything on Facebook or Twitter unless it is under a fake account (a pseudonym) that gives no clue as to your true identity.[1]

The same advice applies to YouTube. When watching apostate videos, it would be worthwhile ensuring that there is zero evidence of "likes" or subscriptions for apostate content visible on a channel that Witness friends, family members or elders can link to you. Again, opening fake accounts solely for this purpose is always a prudent measure.

Without taking the simple precaution of operating under a pseudonym, you are exposing yourself to the very real

---

[1] Facebook tends to clamp down on those who use fake names, which I consider to be extremely insensitive to those who legitimately need to conceal their identity while enjoying access to social media. To lower the risk of having your account closed, the pseudonym you pick should be believable as a real name.

likelihood of your online activity being spotted and used against you. It only takes one slip-up—one "like" or comment in your name attached to the wrong content—for your online activities to have very real consequences, so please exercise extreme care by fiercely protecting your identity!

MANAGE YOUR USE OF BROWSERS AND DEVICES

If you have a believing husband or wife, or if you are in a household with believing family members who could cause you problems if they discovered the extent of your apostasy, as an extra layer of protection it is worthwhile ensuring that no incriminating evidence is left on shared browsers or devices.

The ideal would be for you to have your own dedicated device that nobody else can access—perhaps one that requires a PIN or password to activate. If you are viewing apostate content on a shared computer, tablet or phone that could easily be used by others in your family, you should switch to "incognito" or "private" mode so that nothing is left in the web browser history. Obviously, you would also need to be careful to close your browser window once you have finished!

It is unfortunate that such measures need to be taken, especially if it is a case of concealing your unbelief from a spouse. Such deceptive, sneaky behavior is what you might expect from someone who is covertly viewing pornography online. (I have a friend whose wife, thankfully now awake, was convinced her husband was viewing porn when, on more than one occasion, she would walk into the room and he would instantly close his browser! Though that is precisely what it looked like to her, he was actually debriefing himself on his Witness indoctrination.) As challenging and stressful as the subterfuge may be, awkward situations can hopefully be kept to a minimum if sufficient care is taken.

Exercise Caution with Email

If you are using a fake Facebook account to stay in the loop with your fellow apostates, you will also need a dedicated email address to eliminate the risk of incoming notifications getting you in trouble with believing family members. The same is true if you are using Twitter, or receiving Reddit notifications, or watching YouTube videos from a Google account.

Having set up your email address, you then need to be extremely careful with outgoing emails—especially if you are using multiple email accounts on the same computer or device. I once heard a horror story where an ex-Witness ended up losing his business due to inadvertently emailing a Witness business colleague from an email address that easily identified him as an apostate. (I have made the same mistake myself, thankfully without major ramifications.) Hence, once your dedicated "apostate" email account is up and running, you would do well to exercise caution with both incoming and outgoing messages.

Consider Having an Alibi Ready

It could be that, despite your best efforts, you are confronted by a friend or family member who spots you on an apostate forum, YouTube channel or Facebook group. Perhaps they see you either liking some post or making an approving comment on material that criticizes your former faith.

If the confrontation occurs with your husband or wife, as stressful as it may be you would be well advised to use the opportunity to come clean and have a frank discussion about your doubts and concerns. Marriages rely on trust and honesty, so you would only be causing problems for yourself further down the line by resorting to deception of any kind.

Yes, it may be difficult, even distressing, for you and your spouse to grapple with the shifting parameters of your relationship, especially on the basis of a chance discovery. But by staying calm and expressing yourself with sincerity and empathy for your partner's feelings you should be able to muddle through the situation. (We will be exploring family matters in further detail in the next chapter, including the challenges and dilemmas facing those forced to confront religious differences in a marriage.)

If, however, you are challenged by a family member who needs to be kept in the dark—perhaps a parent or sibling who cannot be reasoned with and who will only cause trouble for you with elders—it may be useful to have an alibi primed and ready with which to extinguish the confrontation. You could say: "I know how this looks, but it's not like that at all. I've been feeling discouraged lately and wanted to prove to myself that I could answer anyone regarding my beliefs, including apostates. I visited this page/group/forum just to see what they're saying, but nothing was in harmony with what we know to be the truth. I've been praying a lot since then and I've decided it was a dangerous move, so I won't be doing anything like that again. I do appreciate the concern, though, and I would want answers from you if I ever caught you doing something similar."

Things may be a little more complicated if you have liked or indicated approval of something that would be considered apostate. You can try, if you wish, suggesting that a "like" was accidental, or that a comment was made with the purpose of starting a conversation that might draw someone back to Jehovah. But depending on the situation, it might be easier to accept your fate by coming clean. When dealing with family members and those you care about, honesty is nearly always the best policy.

UNDERCOVER ACTIVISM

As you spend more time online, you might find yourself gradually drawn into activism. Your Reddit or Facebook posts may get longer. Your Tweets might get more frequent. You may even want to start dabbling in making YouTube videos, perhaps by hiding your appearance, distorting your voice, or making captioned videos. Pretty soon, you have a name and a reputation among other ex-Witnesses even though nobody knows who you are.

This was precisely how I first became involved with activism. I chose the pseudonym "John Cedars" and used this to post blog articles and eventually upload YouTube videos. As exciting, cathartic and fulfilling as this period was, my activities brought with them considerable stress for both me and my wife. The more you express yourself online, the more you risk someone discovering your identity—especially once you begin sharing parts of your story.

It is not impossible to execute a successful fade *and* be an ex-Witness activist, but it can be extremely problematic. In my own case, the longer the subterfuge continued, the more anxious I was to end the charade and out myself, which I eventually did on November 6, 2013 by means of a blog article titled "The Story of Cedars—A Prisoner No More." By December 29, I had been contacted by elders and hauled before a judicial committee, with a print-out of my

blog article (complete with highlighter markings!) presented as evidence of my apostasy.

In summary, though nobody can tell you how to manage
your fade, or at what point you should make a clean break,
you may find the pressure to disassociate will increase the
longer your fade continues, especially if you feel drawn
toward being vocal about your unbelief.

It is a tragedy that Watchtower has engineered this
impossible situation in which you are either totally silent
or at constant risk of discovery and punishment, but until
the organization recognizes how Orwellian it has become
and reforms its shunning policy this is the twisted reality
with which we must come to terms. And it is a reality that
has especially grave ramifications when it comes to family
relationships, as we will now discuss.

CHAPTER SIX

BE REALISTIC WITH YOUR FAMILY

"BLOOD is thicker than water," or so the saying goes. When it comes to cults, however, things are rarely so straightforward. You might entertain the idea that, having learned the disturbing truth about your religion, it is only a matter of time before you succeed in convincing your family to join you in your escape. The problem you have is that there is no magic bullet when it comes to waking someone up from cult indoctrination—especially indoctrination as potent as that found in the Jehovah's Witness faith.

Just as you will have needed time to gradually free yourself from Watchtower's mental grip, so will your family need to shake themselves from their cognitive dissonance at their own pace—assuming they are ready and willing to begin that process at all.

Your husband, wife, son, daughter, brother, sister, mother or father will not reach the conclusion that "Jehovah's organization" is a fraud simply because you have. Even if they have expressed doubts in the past—doubts they have learned to suppress as they "wait on Jehovah"—never underestimate the extent to which Watchtower has ownership of their minds, to the point where they can be turned against you once they learn of your apostasy.

I normally recoil at some of the name-calling that is sometimes employed by ex-Witnesses to heap scorn on the organization. Of course, everyone's sense of humor is different, and there is a lot to be said for exposing cults to mockery and ridicule, but I personally find terms such as "kingdumb hell," "miserable serpent" (instead of ministerial servant) or "washtowel babble and trick society" extremely cringeworthy and juvenile. But there is one such derisive term that hits the nail on the head in neatly explaining the nature of my former religion. You will often hear ex-Witnesses refer to Watchtower, not as "the organization," but as "the Borg."

Any fans of the *Star Trek* science fiction franchise who have escaped Jehovah's Witnesses can instantly see the parallels between the villainous Borg and Watchtower. Just as the Borg are comprised of numerous alien species that have been "assimilated" into serving a "collective," so Jehovah's Witnesses are drawn from various cultures and backgrounds and forced to put on the "new personality"— changing who they are to conform to the organization's requirements.

Borg drones are plugged into a hive mind, stripped of all individuality and changed into heartless beings existing solely for the furtherance of the Borg Queen's agenda, just as Witnesses must comply with the Governing Body's rules and requirements no matter how cruel these may be. Witnesses must sacrifice everything for the sake of advancing "Kingdom interests" to the point of bypassing their humanity if they are required to shun family members or deny their children a life-saving blood transfusion.

The analogy deepens when you observe the difficulty of emancipating someone from the Borg collective. In a *Star Trek: Voyager* episode titled "The Gift," a captured

Borg drone named Seven of Nine fiercely resists attempts to surgically return her to her humanity. "You should have let us die," says Seven to her would-be emancipator, Captain Janeway. "This drone cannot survive outside the collective."

In another tense exchange, after Seven argues that the freedom to be human should include the freedom to go back to being a Borg, Janeway tells her: "You lost the capacity to make a rational choice the moment you were assimilated. They took that from you. And until I'm convinced you've gotten it back, I'm making the choice for you. You're staying here."

"Then you're no different from the Borg," Seven replies.

A devout, committed Jehovah's Witness would be no less adamant in resisting efforts to shake them from their cherished beliefs—beliefs that give them a sense of purpose and have come to define their very existence. Even if you were to present them with incontrovertible evidence that Watchtower has lied to them, or has been responsible for some grave injustice that has caused untold suffering and misery, a totally loyal Witness who is not yet ready to wake up would find reasons to resist your efforts to free them and hate you for even trying.

To stand any chance of waking up a believing relative, you must first assume that they will likely never wake up. You must remember how terrifying and traumatic it was for you when you first embarked on your journey toward unbelief and understand that the same ordeal awaits any who might follow you. You must accept that you were only able to ask the difficult questions and expose yourself to information that turned your entire perception of reality on its head because you were in control of that process every step of the way. It was you who decided what to read, or what videos to watch. You gave yourself permission to look behind the curtain. If that control had been taken from you—if someone else had presumed to tell you what to think or believe—you would have fiercely resisted, retreating deeper into your indoctrination. Why should it be any different for your loved one?

This does not mean you must be passive. There are still things you can do while respecting your dear one's right to awaken in their own good time. Rather than ambushing them with reminders that they are in a cult, which would likely only make things worse, patiently wait for them to approach you for a conversation about your doubts or grievances. If they take their beliefs seriously and care about you, they will come to you sooner or later. They have been manipulated to think that you are at risk of being destroyed at Armageddon unless your spirituality can be salvaged. While it is possible for some relatives to give up all hope and leave you to it, perhaps afraid that if they talk to you their own spirituality will be compromised, a believing husband or wife will likely be especially keen to reach out to you by asking questions aimed at persuading you to return to the meetings. When they do this, you should be ready if your aim is to help them.

At this point I must again qualify my comments by acknowledging that all situations will be different. In some cases you will want to say as little as possible about your unbelief when questioned by family members. For example, if you are a teenager who is working on an exit plan to achieve independence from your parents before gradually fading from the religion, it may be advisable to keep your parents in the dark for as long as possible—especially if you are baptized and there is a chance of being disfellowshipped and kicked out of the house.

If you are married, and you want your husband or wife to join you in your escape (thereby alleviating considerable pressure on your relationship) it is understandable that you would want to seize any opportunity to try to reach through to them. Just remember that, when these opportunities arise, your spouse must feel (and be) in control of the situation if you are to make headway.

ESCAPING AS A MARRIED WITNESS

When you wake up as someone who is married to a believing Witness, you are faced with an extremely difficult situation. Rather than simply walking away, you have added stresses and concerns over how your spouse will be impacted and uncertainty as to whether or not he or she will join you.

In my own case, I was extremely fortunate to have married a woman who does not appreciate being lied to and who values knowing the truth, even if the truth is difficult to stomach. Not long after breaking free from my indoctrination, I set about pursuing a "softly, softly" approach with Dijana, taking great care not to confront her with information if at all possible.

Occasionally, I would discover something that blew me away (such as Watchtower's involvement with the United Nations as an NGO) and my excitement would get the better of me. I simply could not resist letting Dijana know! But at least Dijana could see my sincerity in those instances. The situation was not engineered as a means of manipulating her. Rather, I was genuinely moved by something I had only just learned, and I wanted to share it with my wife and get her thoughts.

Aside from these moments of discovery, I mostly waited for Dijana to initiate conversations about my evaporating faith rather than making her feel backed into a corner. When the very foundation of a marriage is thrown into doubt, it is almost inevitable that both parties will crave dialogue, so I was able to bide my time.

As a still-believing Witness it was Dijana's duty, in her mind, to try to pull her husband from the brink, and whenever these attempts were made I was sure to listen carefully and respond as calmly as possible. In time, these conversations led to Dijana scrutinizing her beliefs and, eventually, she came to join me in my escape. But I have come to appreciate that I was extremely fortunate! Other married Witnesses who seek to flee the organization often end up having a very different experience.

THE DILEMMA OF DIVORCE

It may be that, for whatever reason, your believing spouse simply cannot bring themselves to objectively examine their beliefs. No matter how patient and respectful you are, they view your desertion of the organization as a betrayal and a cause of profound sadness, and—even after many months of inactivity on your part—nothing you say or do can convince them to explore the reasons behind your loss of faith.

If this describes your situation, you have a difficult choice to make. Can you resolve to spend the rest of your life with someone who married you on the assumption that you would always be a Witness?[1] Can you handle spending the

---

[1] It could also be that you are reading this as someone who only got baptized after getting married, or who married someone who later became involved with the Witnesses. Whatever the circumstances, if you have a partner who—despite your best efforts—is not re-

rest of your life with someone who is only in partial control of their own mind? Is your love for your spouse, or their love for you, strong enough to span the chasm that has opened up between you?

Whether to muddle through and stay married or pursue a divorce is a deeply personal decision, and one not to be taken lightly. The stress of facing this dilemma can be overwhelming, and if you are in a position to consult a therapist or marriage guidance counsellor for help during such a situation, you would be well advised to do so. Just be certain that if divorce ends up being the only answer, it is an answer that has been reached after much careful thought and many hours of frank, honest conversations. As in so many difficult situations that arise in a marriage, communication is the key.[2]

CHILD CUSTODY

Naturally, the situation will be further complicated if there are children involved. Custody battles are always traumatic, but the stakes are even higher when one parent is frantically trying to indoctrinate his or her children as loyal cult followers, and the other is desperate to spare them from this fate.

---

motely interested in subjecting their beliefs to scrutiny, you face a considerable dilemma with no easy answers.

[2] If you are anything like me, you will not always find it easy to express yourself verbally, in person, when there is a potentially life-altering issue that needs to be discussed with your mate. When discussing my evaporating faith with Dijana and its ramifications on our marriage, my solution was to communicate in writing. I found that the letter-writing strategy did much to neutralize the emotional tension, giving Dijana space to think about my thoughts and wishes before responding. And, apart from anything else, putting things in writing showed that I was serious.

If this happens to be your unfortunate predicament, you would do well to download a PDF of the Watchtower document "Preparing for Child Custody Cases" (otherwise known as the "Child Custody Packet") which has been compiled as a guide for helping Witness parents win custody battles. As you might expect, the writers follow an "ends justify means" approach and are not above encouraging deception in their efforts to keep children under Watchtower's influence. For example, page 43 of the document coaches a lawyer representing a Witness parent on how to extract the right kind of testimony from young Witnesses, saying:

> Be careful that they don't get the impression that they are in a demonstration at the circuit assembly, when they would show that the first things in life are service and going to the Kingdom Hall. Show hobbies, crafts, social activity, sports, and especially plans for the future. Be careful they don't all say that they are going to be pioneers. Plans can be trade, getting married and having children, journalism, and all kinds of other things. Maybe you can show an interest in art and the theater.

Hence, Watchtower will happily present one image on an assembly or convention platform, but another image entirely in a court of law when it suits their aims. Before your lawyer goes up against such underhanded "theocratic warfare" tactics in the fight for your children, he or she should prepare well. Make sure that if the custody decision goes against you, it is not for want of trying.

After the Divorce

It may be that, once the dust has settled, you find yourself with your marriage in tatters and your children split between one parent trying to raise them to serve Watchtower and another desperate to prevent the organization from impacting future generations. I have received many emails over the years from people in precisely this situation and it can be difficult to know what to say—not least because I have no credentials as a counsellor (nor do I pretend to be one!) and it is impossible to know where to begin when it comes to picking up the pieces, especially when we are talking about a person's life that needs rebuilding.

I can only state the obvious, namely that, in my experience, children do not innately want to be Jehovah's Witnesses—they just want to be children! They want to play games, goof around, get into mischief, and do all the things children enjoy doing. It is certainly not natural for them to spend four hours each week in a windowless building pretending to be interested in something they are generally too young to understand.

If you can offer your child an escape from the monotony of life as a Witness, even if it is only for a brief spell, and make this fleeting experience as enjoyable as possible, you stand a great chance of steering them toward freedom.

Try to be an oasis of calm, happiness and contentment in your child's life. Prove to him or her that you are the exact opposite of the stereotype that Watchtower has carved out for you. You are not overcome by anger and bitterness. You do not leap at every opportunity to lead an immoral, debauched life. You are a principled, upstanding, hard-working parent who offers love and friendship on an unconditional basis. Really, that is all a mother or father needs to be.

No matter what decisions your child makes in the future, they know they can count on you to be there for them. If you make it your goal to show love and kindness at every opportunity, you will make it easier for them to make the right decision. Even if the worst happens, and your child is persuaded to get baptized and start shunning you, at least you will be able to look yourself in the mirror and know that you did your very best to show them a better, kinder, more fulfilled way of living. And your child knows that you will be waiting for them with open arms if they ever change their mind.

Whether you are a parent or not, escaping from Jehovah's Witnesses will usually involve considerable heartache and family upheaval, not to mention the loss of your sense of community. Though you may be left with overwhelming feelings of loneliness due to your decision, it is in your power to win back your sense of belonging and surround yourself with people who love and appreciate you for who you are. In the next chapter, we will discuss ways that you can do precisely that!

CHAPTER SEVEN

BUILD A TEAM

AS A religion, Jehovah's Witnesses pride themselves on show-ing love. They believe that love defines them. The following words at John 13:34, 35, attributed to Jesus, are repeatedly pointed to as describing the affection between Witnesses, which apparently sets them apart as uniquely Christian:

> "I am giving you a new commandment, that you love one another; just as I have loved you, you also love one another. By this all will know that you are my disci-ples—if you have love among yourselves."

Only when you find yourself cast out of Jehovah's Wit-nesses do you discover just how hollow this claim is. Even when still inside the religion, love among fellow believers can turn out to be little more than a thin veneer. For example, it does not take much to find yourself preemptively shunned as "bad association" simply by failing to attend meetings.

I saw firsthand just how fickle the "brotherly love" among Witnesses can be when, in 2010, I began distancing myself from the organization while still a baptized member. Before I stopped attending meetings I had been playing football (soccer) on most Sunday afternoons with friends from my Kingdom Hall. As soon as it became apparent that I was frequently absent from meetings, I found myself frozen out of recreational activities.[1] Apparently, by failing

---

[1] Bizarrely, while inactive I would still occasionally receive invita-tions to congregation get-togethers, held periodically at a local

to be in a certain place by a certain time each week, I was now "bad association"—a destructive influence who would corrupt the "useful habits" of my brothers if I were to join them in kicking a ball around a field.

It can be unnerving to discover just how shallow and conditional the love between Jehovah's Witnesses truly is. So long as you acknowledge the authority of the Governing Body and demonstrate this by doing and saying all the right things, you can expect to be showered with affection. But the moment you fall short of what is required of you, the love can vanish almost instantly. Hence, when you set about escaping from the organization, it is almost inevitable that you will experience social isolation even before you make your exit official, and this can take its toll emotionally.

We humans are social creatures. We thrive on interacting with our kind. We hate to feel lonely and isolated and we become angry and frustrated when we receive the "cold shoulder treatment." It is for these reasons that ostracism, or shunning, is such an effective means of punishment. We are simply not programmed to handle being ignored or rejected. That is why, when escaping from Jehovah's Witnesses, it is important to set about building a replacement community, or "team," as soon as possible.

"Easier said than done," you might be thinking! As Jehovah's Witnesses, we never really had to exert too much effort when it came to making friends. The organization insists on compulsory friendship between believers, all of whom are considered fit for association no matter what

---

community hall. Apparently, it was acceptable for me to eat and dance side-by-side with the congregation (perhaps as a gesture of goodwill and charity) but running up and down a field with them on Sunday afternoons was something else entirely.

eccentricities or character flaws they may have. You could be the craziest, most antisocial person imaginable, but if you become a Jehovah's Witness and attend all the meetings while steering clear of any incriminating behavior, you can effectively demand that everyone in the congregation spend time with you as your friend.

Looking back, it is no surprise to me that, in each of the three congregations of which I have been a member during my years as a Witness, there was a sizable complement of eccentric, socially-challenged members with whom I would dread being paired in the door-to-door work—their mere presence beside me on the doorstep being a major handicap in my efforts to advertise my faith to total strangers. It seems obvious in retrospect that an organization insisting on compulsory friendship will attract people who would otherwise find it extremely difficult to make friends.

Thankfully, once free of Watchtower's mental grip, you can no longer be told who your friends must be. You are free to choose from among people with attributes to which you feel personally drawn. And when you allow yourself to embrace as friends those whom you previously looked down on as dreaded "worldly" folk, you discover that many of them are fine, moral, decent individuals who anyone would feel privileged to count as friends. It is from among such well-rounded, uplifting, sincere people that you can now set about building your team. The question is: where to find them?

Even while still inside the organization, perhaps in the early stages of implementing your fade, you can start making reconnaissance forays into your local community and figuring out ways of integrating yourself into society. Perhaps you could start with your non-believing relatives. Are there any who might be sympathetic to your plight, and can be counted on to discreetly support you? Perhaps you might have neighbors, old high school buddies or workmates to whom you can similarly reach out.

Are there any local sports teams, gym classes or walking clubs you can join? Does your local college have any study courses you could sign up for? Are there any local soup kitchens or aid charities in need of volunteers? These are all excellent ways of engaging with your community, meeting people and expanding your social circle. And now that you have freed yourself of Watchtower's hang-ups surrounding "bad association" and "worldly holidays," there is nothing stopping you from finally saying "yes" to your workmates when they invite you to the office Christmas party!

As you begin to make new friends (or establish stronger friendships with non-believing relatives, neighbors and acquaintances you knew previously as a Witness), you will need to decide how many details about your Witness background you wish to divulge.

It might be helpful to have a small nucleus of individuals who are sympathetic to your predicament and can offer you moral support and a listening ear, especially as you navigate the potential unpleasantness and hostility that lies ahead as you distance yourself from the organization. However, do not expect everyone you encounter to understand your plight, and certainly do not allow yourself to feel unduly disheartened or offended if you do not get the sympathy you would hope for.

The cultish world that you are leaving behind is completely alien to what many people can comprehend, and some of your new friends may feel ill-equipped to offer an opinion on something that is clearly deeply personal to you without knowing much about a religion that, frankly, may not interest them.

Some will regard religion as a taboo—a complex, profound, divisive topic that they simply cannot relate to or bring themselves to talk about. If someone reacts indifferently to your story, this does not necessarily mean they are a bad person or unworthy of your friendship. You can still find their company uplifting and a welcome distraction from what is going on elsewhere in your life even if it is understood that any talk of religion is a "buzzkill" for some.

Even so, it would be advisable to recruit at least some friends who take an interest in your background and can be supportive during the difficulties and challenges you are going through. You do not need experience in the Witness faith to understand that breaking apart families through shunning is wrong, or that there is nothing moral about covering up child abuse or persuading people to die rather than accept blood transfusions. There are people out there in your community who will want to show solidarity with your plight, and it is only a matter of time before you find them. It is simply a matter of putting forth effort.

Of course, few will understand your predicament better than other ex-Witnesses, and you will find a ready supply of them online. For example, the "Ex-Jehovah's Witness Recovery Group 3" on Facebook (https://www.facebook.com/groups/xjwrg3) has over 11,000 members, at the time of writing, and is a great place to share your story and get support. (Please bear in mind my advice in Chapter Five before testing the water on Facebook.) Alternatively, you will find that the ex-JW Reddit page, (https://www.reddit.com/r/exjw) with over 20,000 members (and rapidly growing!), offers a supportive environment in which ex-Witnesses can post about their experiences anonymously and receive helpful advice.

As you meet other ex-Witnesses online, there will inevitably be opportunities to attend meet-ups and social gatherings where you will have the chance to interact in person with those who have had an almost identical experience to yours. I have attended dozens of these events in different countries, and generally found them to be fun and uplifting occasions. It can be a tremendous psychological boost to be surrounded by fellow apostates who automatically relate to what you have been through without requiring an exhaustive introduction to Witness beliefs and culture.

The more you attend meet-ups and get to know other ex-Witnesses online, the more you will find yourself drawn to particular individuals with whom you have something in common other than your shared religious background. But just because someone has the same former religion as you, this does not automatically make them friend material. If someone was unpleasant or antisocial as a Witness, they will usually continue to be those things as an ex-Witness.

Some ex-Witnesses seem to naively assume that, on leaving Watchtower behind, they have now joined a grand ex-Witness collective, or surrogate organization, where everyone must be friends or else they are guilty of shunning and therefore replicating the evils of their former faith. But this is not how things work in the real world. Finding friends involves more than simply identifying people who have something in common with you. Everyone is different, and not everyone deserves a place in your team.

It is ok, even necessary, to unfriend or block other ex-Witnesses on social media if they turn out to be vindictive and unkind, or start to behave abusively either toward you or others. Unfortunately, some ex-Witnesses seem to revel in stirring controversy and/or character-assassinating those who do not meet with their approval. You are not "disfellowshipping" or "shunning" such ones by no longer granting them space on your phone, tablet or computer screen. You are simply deciding who your friends are. You have the absolute right to manage your social media experience, and you should not feel compelled to entertain individuals who insist on projecting their bitterness and negativity on everyone else.

Though it is almost inevitable that you will have hostile encounters and difficult exchanges with other ex-Witnesses, try not to let these experiences dishearten you, or put you off from including ex-Witnesses in your circle of friends. By chatting with ex-Witnesses on Skype, meeting certain ones for a drink or having them over for dinner, you may find that their sense of humor or kind, accommodating personality makes them a perfect fit for your growing post-JW team.

With patience and persistence, and perhaps some degree of trial and error, before long you will hopefully find that the community you lost has been entirely rebuilt and is better than anything you had previously! Rather than conditional love and compulsory friendships being the norm, you are now part of a tight-knit unit that has your back—and it is a beautiful, diverse group of remarkable individuals. They are different people with different ideas, beliefs and backgrounds. Some team members can relate directly to your cult experience having been through it themselves. Others are less familiar with what it means to have a religion dictate one's life, but they can still offer love, support and solidarity—perhaps in ways that your ex-Witness friends cannot. The one thing they all have in common is that they love and appreciate you for who you are—not for what an organization insists you should be!

Even so, as rewarding as it will be to have your social life back up and running, you may still find there is something missing. If, despite the support and understanding of your friends and loved ones, you still find yourself consumed with uncertainty, anxiety and despair as a result of your cult experience, I would urgently recommend that you seek the services of a mental health professional. The next chapter will offer a few tips for finding the help you need.

CHAPTER EIGHT

SEEKING PROFESSIONAL HELP

NO MATTER how smoothly your escape goes, it is very likely that you will experience considerable anxiety and emotional distress as a result of your decision to exit. In addition to pressure being put on you by Witness elders, friends and family members (who may subject you to scorn and attempts at coercing you to stay), you may also struggle to cope with the residual trauma from years of Watchtower fear-mongering, manipulation and sexual repression.

Because I am not a trained therapist, and because everyone is different, I am in no position to guide you when it comes to emotional and psychological healing. But if you are struggling mentally and emotionally as a result of your experience, perhaps battling feelings of hopelessness and despair, you would be well advised to urgently seek professional help.[1] As Bonnie Zieman, a professional psychotherapist (who also happens to be an ex-Witness), wrote in her excellent book *Exiting the JW Cult: A Healing Handbook for Current & Former Jehovah's Witnesses*:

---

[1] This might include relationship and marriage counseling if you have a husband or wife, especially if there is a very real risk of the collapse of your marriage due to exiting the Witnesses. If you deeply love your spouse, you will want to do everything possible to keep your relationship intact, and relationship counsellors are trained to give you the impartial, non-judgmental help you need.

You must take responsibility for meeting your psychological needs and get actual professional help when needed. Chronic severe depression, unmanageable anxiety, panic attacks, uncontrollable or persistent anger issues, etc. would be indicators that you need the help of a mental health professional.

It could be that you feel the need to seek professional help, but cannot imagine being able to afford it. Most countries are slowly beginning to grasp the importance of making mental health services more accessible, but there is still a great deal of work to be done. For example, in the United Kingdom, doctors can prescribe free counseling paid for by the National Health Service, but the waiting list (at the time of writing) can mean a delay of many months before you actually get to sit down with a trained professional. Other countries or states may have similar limitations depending on the demand for available resources.

Even so, it would be worthwhile exploring all possible avenues for getting seen by somebody who can help steer you to a better emotional place. Elsewhere in her book, Zieman writes:

> If money is a consideration, you can try to find a university, university hospital, or a psychotherapy training center where student therapists, about to graduate, are beginning to see clients. Because they are still students and need to practice their new skills with actual clients, they sometimes offer their services at reduced rates or even on a sliding scale based on your ability to pay. While they may not be versed in cult deprogramming techniques, they will provide a non-judgmental ear and some tried-and-true ways to manage your anxiety.

If you have exhausted all attempts at finding professional help and none is available, or the costs are prohibi-

tive, try to at least find someone who can listen empatheti-
cally to your story. When I interviewed Zieman for my John
Cedars channel, I asked her what an ex-Witness could do to
debrief themselves. She answered:

> If they can, they need to find some way to talk about it.
> So, if they have someone else who's come out with them
> or if they have relatives or friends who were never a
> JW—now you don't want to overwhelm the poor person
> with everything, and you've got to be judicious in terms
> of how you do it—but that's the way we as humans heal.

This takes us back to what we discussed in the previous
chapter about building a team. Your team is anyone who
values you for who you are, and who can provide support
and solidarity during times of crisis. Even if you cannot find
a mental health professional, you would do well to at least
have someone on your team who can give you a listening ear.
Finding the right person may take time and patience, especially as you slowly rebuild your social life and integrate yourself in your local community, but it is by no means impossible.

Whether you can afford professional help or not, you
would also do well to read books that have been specifically
written for helping ex-cult members cope emotionally with
their exit. Zieman has written a number of excellent books
along these lines, all of which are available on Amazon. One
in particular, *Cracking the Cult Code for Therapists: What Every
Cult Victim Wants Their Therapist to Know*, is specifically written
to brief therapists with limited understanding of cults so that
they can give you more personalized treatment.[2] *Take Back*

---

[2] Unfortunately, not all therapists will have experience and knowledge when it comes to cult deprogramming. There is still considerable work to be done in raising awareness of cult mind control in
the mental health community. However, as Bonnie Zieman noted
when I raised this issue with her in our video interview, therapists

Your Life: Recovering from Cults and Abusive Relationships by Janja Lalich and Madeleine Tobias is also highly recommended.

If you are battling depression and anxiety as a result of your years as a Witness, one thing you must never do is ignore the problem altogether in the hope that it will correct itself. If there is a concerned friend who you can speak to, speak to them. If you need to vent on the ex-JW sub-Reddit page, or on an ex-JW Facebook group, please do so. If there is professional therapy available to you, either freely or affordably, sign up for it. If there are books that will help you to untangle the feelings of loss, guilt, anger or betrayal, read them and apply their advice.

If your thoughts become so dark that you begin to contemplate suicide, be sure to reach out to someone—anyone! It can be someone you know, or someone on a suicide prevention hotline.[3] Just do whatever it takes to weather the storm and live to fight another day. Find a way to make the best of the rare and precious gift of life, and deprive Watchtower the chance to add to the long list of victims who have tragically succumbed to its cruel, inhumane teachings and practices.[4]

---

are still trained to help you manage feelings of loss, grief and anger. "It doesn't matter where the loss comes from," she said. "If you're dealing with loss, if you're grieving, any good therapist can help you with that process." In addition to her book *Cracking the Cult Code for Therapists*, Bonnie has documents freely available for download on her website BonnieZieman.com. They offer invaluable guidance for therapists if their lack of knowledge about cults becomes an issue.

[3] The following suicide prevention numbers can be dialed if you need someone to talk to: National Suicide Hotline (USA): 1 800 273 8255, National Suicide Hotline (Canada): 1 800 448 1833, Samaritans (UK): 08457 90 90 90, Samaritans (Ireland): 1850 60 90 90, Lifeline (Australia): 13 11 14, Lifeline (New Zealand): 0800 543 354.

[4] Unfortunately we have no way of knowing just how many have committed suicide due to Watchtower's cruel shunning policy, but there is anecdotal evidence pointing to a horrifying bodycount. Ev-

It is also important to be realistic. Do not demand too much of yourself. In my experience, there is no "reset" button a person can push to purge themselves entirely of all emotional side effects caused by prolonged exposure to a group like Jehovah's Witnesses. Rather than chasing a mirage of false hope by assuming that you can completely reverse the effects of involvement with the Witnesses if you can only read the right book or connect with the right therapist, it would be more realistic to seek to reconcile what has happened in such a way that you can move forward.

Like it or not, the religion is part of your past, and therefore a part of who you are. It may be that you have been scarred emotionally by your experience, but it is up to you to decide whether the scar will be a cause of shame, anger and bitterness, or a badge of honor—proof that you have been through a traumatizing experience and have emerged stronger.

Try, wherever possible, to reach a point where you can turn a negative into a positive by using your ordeal to make you a better person, either by reaching out to raise awareness through respectful, positive activism, or by being a source of kindness and empathy when you encounter other cult victims, or those who have been through a similarly traumatic experience. Turn your pain into a source of strength from which others can draw.

Whatever it takes to gain mastery over your inner troubles, the time, tears and persistence will be worth it eventually. With patience and resolve you will arrive at a point

ery year, JWsurvey.org runs a global survey of current and former Jehovah's Witnesses. In the 2016 survey, 31% of respondents (1,113 individuals) claimed to have contemplated or attempted suicide as a result of being a part of the Jehovah's Witness organization.

where you can stop looking back and start to look forward. Until then, draw comfort from knowing that time is on your side and a happy, meaningful life of freedom awaits!

CHAPTER NINE

TAKE YOUR TIME AND ENJOY YOUR FREEDOM!

IN THE previous chapters, we explored the various challenges facing someone who decides to escape from Jehovah's Witnesses. As we near the end of our discussion, hopefully you feel more confident about the journey ahead. Although there is no easy way to extricate yourself from Jehovah's Witnesses, there are certainly ways that you can make leaving more difficult. By avoiding these wherever possible, you stand a much better chance of moving on from your experience.

Even though there will likely be difficulties ahead, perhaps even pain and heartache, it is nothing you cannot handle. As you embark on this journey and weave your way through the minefield of obstacles and pitfalls Watchtower has laid before you, it is important to remember that time is on your side and you are now in control.

When you were a Jehovah's Witness, the Armageddon clock was constantly ticking. You never knew when the end was going to come and you were determined that your service to Jehovah would not be found wanting when Jesus and his angels brought their wave of fiery destruction on the earth.

A Witness has endless tasks to complete and goals to pursue. It is not enough to merely attend a meeting, they must also prepare well for it. It is not enough to be actively involved in preaching the "good news," they must be putting in as many hours as possible to the extent of pioneering if their circumstances allow. A Witness must give everything for Jehovah and his organization. There can be no allowance for taking one's time or being half-hearted in service.

But once you decide to free yourself from Watchtower's control, the dynamic changes entirely. Nobody is holding a stopwatch and insisting that you hasten your exit. No awards are handed out for the quickest or most successful fade, or the most spectacular disassociation. Just as getting involved in a religion is (or should be) an extremely personal, intimate process—so is the process of extricating yourself from a belief system to which you can no longer subscribe. In short, you get to do this on your own terms and according to your own timescale. Do not let anyone tell you otherwise!

It could be that you are awakened to the reality that the Jehovah's Witness religion is not true, but you are not yet in a position to begin your fade. Perhaps you are an elder or a Bethelite and, due to being so deeply embedded in the organization, you would immediately attract problems for yourself if you were to begin fading. This is a common scenario and you are well within your rights to carry on as normal for the time being until the time is right to begin implementing your exit plan.

Alternatively, it could be that you are an elder's wife, or the spouse of an extremely zealous Witness. Nobody is demanding that you begin stirring up friction in your relationship by skipping meetings and scaling down your time in service. Be patient. Take as much time as you need to weigh your situation and make whatever decisions need to be made. Freedom from Jehovah's Witnesses is not a moving target. It will still be waiting for you no matter how slow your escape is, and it will be all the richer and more satisfying for being won in a way that meets your needs to the extent possible.

When the day finally comes for you to breathe a sigh of relief, knowing that you can put your Witness experience behind you and begin living your life authentically, you might find yourself revisiting the question posed in the first chapter. Yes, you have now escaped from Jehovah's Witnesses, but what next? Where will you "go to" in terms of your belief system? Will you remain a Christian, or embrace a non-Christian set of beliefs, or do away with religion altogether? This, again, is *entirely your call*. Nobody gets to tell you that you *must* follow a particular way of thinking.

You will surely have sacrificed a great deal and been through no small amount of emotional upheaval in the process of emancipating yourself from the Witnesses. You did not put yourself through such an ordeal simply to wind up in another closed-minded group where you are not free to ask questions and reach your own conclusions on matters of faith, belief and conscience.

In my own case, my journey to freedom eventually led me to agnostic atheism. Agnostic atheists do not assert that there is no God, as gnostic atheists do.[1] They simply say that there is no compelling reason to believe in any

---

[1] When most people criticize atheism as dogmatic and a form of religion, they usually have gnostic atheists in mind. This is not entirely unreasonable, because insisting that there is no "God" of any kind when his (or its) existence cannot be proven or disproven is an unsupportable truth claim. Though I am sure that gnostic atheists must exist, in my years of atheism up to writing this book I have yet to meet one.

deity or follow any particular system of worship, but they are willing to consider any evidence of the divine that may become available if it meets the burden of proof. (Or, as Carl Sagan was so fond of saying: "Extraordinary claims require extraordinary evidence.")

Though I find this a reasonable position to take respecting religion, I do not expect everyone to join me in embracing atheism. I have come to accept that religion is a part of society that is here to stay. It is only a question of trying to make sure religious groups and organizations do as little harm as possible. If people are comforted or consoled by religious ideas, it is not my place to insist otherwise.

I am occasionally told that, by being open about my atheism, I am robbing people of hope and jeopardizing their spirituality. My response to this accusation is that, as an activist, it is not my job to tell people what to believe on leaving a harmful cult, just as a firefighter who plucks someone from their burning home is not responsible for building them a new one. A person's religious views are deeply personal and cannot be dictated by others. You are free to decide for yourself what to believe and what not to believe. I would only recommend that, whatever your beliefs end up being, they are the result of asking questions and devoting time to careful thought and introspection.

It is not unheard of for ex-Witnesses to immediately get themselves entangled in another cult or cult-like group, and it is not hard to envision how this might happen. When you go through the emotional upheaval of leaving a religion, especially if this involves the pain of ostracism by family members, you are more vulnerable to manipulation by other groups offering you a sense of community and that reassuring, seductive feeling of total certainty.

You may not feel that you are in a weakened state or susceptible to coercion, but try not to become too complacent. Just as a patient needs to take it easy and not overexert themselves while recovering from extensive surgery, you would be well advised to rest up and convalesce intellectually before attaching yourself to some other religion or way of thinking, especially one that insists on exclusivity or discourages any questioning of established dogma.

You have all the time in the world to explore and compare various religious, philosophical or scientific schools of thought, and there is no deadline for settling on your new post-Witness outlook. Since escaping the Witnesses, the Armageddon clock has stopped ticking and it is no longer a question of throwing every minute of your time into the one true divinely approved belief system so as to avoid annihilation!

Revel in the process of learning, assimilating information and absorbing different views and ideas. This, after all, is how we grow as people. Even if we deeply disagree with a certain set of views, there is no harm in familiarizing ourselves with them if only to better understand how others think and what motivates them. Only by hearing the arguments of others can you test your own ideas and find out whether they stand up to scrutiny.

You will find that there is a great sense of satisfaction and fulfillment to be found in engaging respectfully and non-judgmentally with others, embracing diversity of thought, expanding your knowledge and broadening your perspective. This, after all, is what true intellectual freedom is about—being able to challenge your convictions and go wherever the evidence takes you.

Another challenge facing you, once you are free, is that of rebuilding your sense of community. It could be that you are so disheartened by your abandonment by Witness friends and family that you are reticent to pursue building future relationships due to the fear of being rejected all over again. On the other hand, it could be that you are impatient to rebuild your social circle, to the point where you feel upset when others do not reciprocate your efforts at starting a friendship.

Whatever the precise nature of the challenge, do not give up on yourself and, again, be patient! Though you may have been burned by your experience with the Witnesses, time is on your side and there is no reason to feel pressured.

It may be that you need time to overcome your insecurities, perhaps with the help of a professional therapist. There is always an element of trial and error when you are emotionally opening yourself up to others. Though there will almost inevitably be disappointments ahead, with seemingly promising friendships not turning out the way you had hoped, do not give up! You might deprive yourself of some truly beautiful relationships if you are unwilling to take the rough with the smooth and expose yourself to a few risks.

Conversely, if you are dismayed at your lack of progress in expanding your social circle, try to be realistic. Good friends are not always easy to come across. It may take some time before you can settle on a group of friends who value and appreciate you for who you are. As we discussed in Chapter Seven, if you are persistent and pursue opportunities to meet people locally, you will increase the likelihood of encountering sincere, uplifting people and building a team that has your back.

Occasionally, you might be haunted by reminders of the world you left behind. A former Witness friend or family member might send you an emotional message designed to guilt-trip you into returning to the fold. Try not to lash out or let it upset you. Remember that the person is not fully in possession of their own mind. They are more likely to one day wake up if you can respond with kindness and respect—assuming you feel the need to respond at all.

Ultimately, the best answer to Witnesses who may look down on you for leaving what you once considered to be "the truth" is to lead a happy, fulfilled life free from bitterness or resentment. This is especially true if you are a parent of children who are being raised in the religion, perhaps by a believing ex-spouse. Rather than pressuring them into joining you in your escape, thereby living up to the apostate stereotype of being manipulative, show your children how contented and meaningful your life is now that you are free from Watchtower's control.

While their believing parent will almost inevitably be a demanding influence in their lives, trying to shape their thinking and behavior at every turn, you get to be the exact opposite—a sanctuary of peace and intellectual freedom where they can find momentary shelter from the prudish, judgmental attitudes and closed-mindedness intrinsic to the Witness faith. In time, if they feel you are dignifying them with the freedom to decide for themselves, they are more likely to follow your lead than confine themselves to a life that is hopelessly restrictive and greatly at odds with the emotional and developmental needs of young people.[2]

---

[2] Of course, you are well within your rights to pursue legal action with the aim of blocking your ex from indoctrinating your children as Jehovah's Witnesses if you have the means and opportunity to

Perhaps the greatest challenge you face in escaping Jehovah's Witnesses is to reach a point where you can forgive yourself for getting dragged in to begin with. When you leave the Witnesses it is easy to be fiercely angry at yourself for being so easily conned into believing something that is manifestly ludicrous when subjected to the mildest scrutiny. You might wonder: "How could I have genuinely believed that billions of people deserve to die for not believing as I do? How could I have prayed for this to happen every day?"

Try not to capitulate to self-loathing in this way. You did not get sucked into this absurd belief system willingly and knowingly, or as a result of being stupid or gullible. You got sucked in because you were lied to. Even the smartest people can be persuaded to believe things that do not make sense if they are indoctrinated as children or cleverly tricked and deceived as adults. It is important that you can reach a stage where you can forgive yourself for the years or decades you may have wasted in the organization and seize whatever positives can be gleaned from your experience.

In my own case, my experience has put me in a position where I know more than most people about cults, making it

do so. I do occasionally hear of instances where this strategy pays off. But, especially if it means adding stress and expense to what will already be an exhausting custody battle, it is worth weighing the pros and cons carefully when deciding how to proceed. Watchtower indoctrination is extremely potent and your children deserve to be spared it wherever possible, but there is also something to be said for dodging accusations of being an unyielding parent who is unwilling to let their children reach their own decisions. Simply by having one parent who is awakened and free, your children stand an excellent chance of avoiding a life dominated by Watchtower manipulation.

easier for me to show solidarity and compassion to victims of such groups and motivating me to raise awareness of their plight through activism. I also met my wife as a direct result of being heavily involved with the Witnesses, and the happy marriage and beautiful daughter that have resulted from this encounter are unquestionably products of my Witness past. There is no shame in admitting that.

Of course, none of this excuses the abuse inflicted on countless Witnesses by Watchtower, and it certainly does not make Witness teachings true. But, for better or worse, I am the person I am because of once being a Jehovah's Witness, and I have found it extremely beneficial to take ownership of this fact and make peace with my past in order to move forward.

It may be difficult or impossible, even with therapy, to fully cleanse oneself of lingering emotional and psychological damage from years of being in a cult, but it is possible and extremely enriching to reconcile your past experiences and embrace the fact that you are a stronger, wiser, more compassionate person as a result of your Witness background. If there is any pot of gold at the end of the rainbow once your bid for freedom is successful, it is attaining a state of mind where you are free from guilt and self-loathing, and able to love yourself for dealing with everything life has thrown at you as best you could.

Yes, you have made some bad choices in life. Who hasn't?! Yes, you have wasted time and energy supporting and promoting an abusive organization, perhaps over many years. But while millions of Witnesses continue to languish in servitude to the whims of a group of men in New York, you are one of the few who summoned the bravery and integrity to go against the flow; to question cherished beliefs and value truth above all else. Never allow yourself to forget that!

No matter what challenges await you, you get to look at yourself in the mirror and know that you beat the odds, triumphed over adversity, and won a life that is authentic. You may not have all the answers, but you now have something infinitely more valuable. You have the freedom to ask questions. The freedom to think for yourself. The freedom to be loved and appreciated unconditionally. The freedom to be you.

POSTSCRIPT

WHILE preparing *How to Escape From Jehovah's Witnesses*, I gave supporters of the project on Indiegogo the opportunity to publish their stories of breaking free from abusive cults. I felt this would be a fitting and uplifting way to conclude the book, because by presenting numerous examples of those who have successfully escaped Jehovah's Witnesses and similar groups, the light at the end of the tunnel would seem that little bit brighter for those hoping to get out. And so, here follows the stories of a number of brave individuals who have found happiness and fulfillment by extricating themselves from a controlling, cult-like movement.

JACQUELINE SHAW

Jacqueline was born into a Witness family going back three generations on her mother's side. Her parents took the religion very seriously. "My sister and I were raised extremely strict and harshly, even by JW standards," Jacqueline recalls. "We never missed a Saturday out in field service, nor Sunday. And, we attended meetings even when we traveled on vacation."

Eager to meet her parents' expectations, Jacqueline began auxiliary pioneering while still in high school and pioneered for three years after graduating. Despite giving her best in pursuit of "Kingdom interests," Jacqueline was frustrated with pioneering. "I became frustrated with barely making ends meet with my meager earnings. I also was aware of how much time we all knowingly wasted by just driving around in order to count time," she says.

After much soul-searching, Jacqueline resolved to quit pioneering for a while so that she could improve her earning potential as a pioneer by attending college. But this news did not go down well with her parents. "I was promptly informed I needed to move out of the house for this decision," Jacqueline recalls. "To add insult to injury, my parents refused to talk to me after I moved out—all because I had chosen to go to college."

By the time Jacqueline had received her qualification—a double master's in Business—she had figured out that the organization was entirely unworthy of her devotion. She quit attending meetings and has since gone on to found a number of thriving businesses.

"Looking back, I remember thinking that at age 21 I had lost three years of my life and how 'old' I was going back to school," Jacqueline says. "I feel so badly for those that were awakened so many years beyond that and gave their youth to this cult."

Michael Bryson

Michael was 18 and already having doubts about God when his Jehovah's Witness social life was unexpectedly turned on its head. His congregation was split in two and he found himself assigned to a different congregation than that of his childhood friends.

"Meetings suddenly became disorienting and alien, and social interactions before and after were excruciating," Michael recalls. "Being bureaucratically and autocratically transferred to a new 'unit' felt like losing something of myself."

In an effort to salvage something of his waning faith, Michael tried attending his friends' congregation, but was made to feel like a rebel. "The Witnesses have a wonderfully passive-aggressive way of noting when you are out of line, or failing to conform to expectations," Michael says. "I was thanked for 'visiting' and asked how things were going in my 'new' congregation—an unsubtle way of telling me that I did not belong there anymore."

But rather than fall in line, Michael came up with a radical solution to his predicament: he stopped going to meetings and moved to a different city 30 miles away. The fresh start was exactly what he needed. Having slipped off his elders' radar, Michael had the freedom to expand his knowledge by burying himself in books—both the writings of Ray Franz, and literature by the likes of Proust and Dante. Michael also saw for himself that "worldly" people, including gay waiters and bookstore clerks whom he befriended, were not the loathsome individuals he had been warned about.

Today, thanks to his insatiable appetite for learning and refusal to succumb to Watchtower's warnings about higher education, Michael is professor of English Literature at Cal State, Northridge. He is relieved and grateful that inflexibility by elders in his youth had the unintended effect of putting him onto the road to freedom.

ADRIENNE

Having been born with autism, Adrienne did not begin life with glowing prospects. But it certainly did not help that her mother was contacted by Jehovah's Witnesses

on the day she stepped out of the maternity ward. As a result, Adrienne began a Witness upbringing lacking in joy and stimulation. "As a toddler I remember the unutterable boredom of study routines spent counting the joints under those infernal green chairs," she says.

Adrienne struggled with doubts and frustrations as a Witness youth. After a failed marriage to a non-Witness left her caring for a child by herself, she decided to take the religion seriously and agreed to a Bible study. But once returned to the fold, her torment was only beginning. She married a ministerial servant who "physically, psychologically and emotionally" abused her.

"When I began to report incidents around 1990, which included him smashing my head against a wall, attempted strangulations, the fingerprints of which I camouflaged for meetings, I wasn't believed," Adrienne says. "According to the two witness rule and the elder's manual, women and vulnerable people don't matter in the Witness patriarchal and hierarchical system even though I had documentary evidence from legal bodies."

Adrienne got a separation from her husband and they were finally divorced, but despite her best efforts she was never made to feel accepted by her congregation. "The love they talk about is superficial unless you're privileged to be in a prominent family or clique," she says.

Adrienne has since escaped her Witness indoctrination and recently celebrated her first Christmas. Having learned of Watchtower's track record of abuse and cover-ups, she finally feels at peace. "Don't be conned by the propaganda saying you will be sad, miserable and mentally diseased," Adrienne advises. "Take courage. Life's good out here!"

SVEN

Sven's path to mental freedom began when his young daughters expressed an interest in celebrating birthdays. His search for a meaningful, rational answer to the rejection of birthday celebrations by Jehovah's Witnesses left him empty-handed and confused.

As Sven expanded his search to other topics, cracks in his beliefs started to appear. "Since I'm especially interested in history I could not get past the obvious fault of the 607 B.C.E. teaching," he explains. "That really bothered me."

When Sven approached the elders over his growing doubts, he found their advice uninspiring. "The elders were at first very helpful," he says. "But when my knowledge grew their arguments ended in a simple solution of just increase my personal study, meeting attendance and field service."

Sven's hunger to learn more eventually led him to "lurk" on apostate forums, where he began to see for himself that the majority ex-Witness activists are not the angry, bitter miscreants of whom he had been warned. After reading *Crisis of Conscience* and *The Gentile Times Reconsidered*, he came to realize the true nature of the organization and has been distancing himself ever since.

At the time of writing, Sven senses a judicial committee is imminent as he observes the resolve of his elders "to clean out inactive ones" who might be showing signs of no longer believing. Despite anxiousness over what lies in store, Sven is glad to have shown his daughters the joy and contentment that comes with making a conscientious stand for truth.

ETHAN SPENCER

Ethan's earliest memories as a Jehovah's Witness include rejection and ostracism. Having been born out of wedlock to a disfellowshipped mother who was shunned throughout his infancy, he knew it would be an uphill struggle to find friendship and acceptance.

"I wasn't allowed to foster any 'worldly' connections, so I grew up isolated," Ethan says. "I was trapped between a world I wasn't allowed to be a part of and an organization that I felt wanted nothing to do with me."

After leaving high school, Ethan found his options were severely restricted by his upbringing. "When I left I had nothing to fall back on so I had to work a lot of menial jobs to get where I am today without a degree."

Deprived of the chance to pursue higher education, Ethan struggled with feelings of hopelessness. "I have a massive inferiority complex that has led me down many dark paths, some within striking distance of ending my life," Ethan says. "I sometimes wonder what I could have been had I never been raised a part of the JW organization: always being admonished to reach for higher and higher goals in a group I had no interest in."

Finally, after years of gradually drifting from the organization, Ethan attended his last meeting in 2010. He has since moved a number of times and appears to have successfully faded. Despite frustration at the negative impact of his Witness upbringing, Ethan is relieved to have escaped. "I can say that being raised a JW has ruined my relationships, my mental health, my job prospects, and has left many a scar that I still feel today," he admits. "However, despite all of this, and because of it, I have never been happier than I am now to be away from it."

NICHOLE KYCIA

Nichole was seven when her mother began studying with a Jehovah's Witness coworker. When the family started attending meetings, Nichole was in constant fear for her father—an unbeliever. "Every single day I would pray that my father would learn the truth and not be killed at Armageddon," she recalls.

Against her father's objections, Nichole was baptized at 15. "I now consider that to be the biggest mistake in my life," she admits. Despite busying herself in the congregation as an auxiliary pioneer, Nichole's doubts grew as she absorbed knowledge at school. By the time she was 18, she had rebelled.

"The sexual repression and lack of sexual education quickly led to a teen pregnancy," she recalls. "I was swiftly disfellowshipped and shunned by my family." Fortunately, her boyfriend's family took her in, allowing her to finish high school and pursue higher education.

Before long, Nichole was married. She even managed to have more children while studying for her Master's Degree, and finally landed her dream job as a physician assistant in pediatrics. "When I finished my first week I cried, literally, tears of joy, because I know that I got out just in time," Nichole says. "So many others miss out on that opportunity for an education and for a rewarding career."

Nichole was later reinstated, but found herself shunned by her Witness family once she began fading. After continued struggles with hang-ups over Armageddon, she eventually found mental freedom by applying herself to objective research. "I found that once I was no longer restricted in what I could read the world opened up before me and everything became so clear," she says. "Once a person looks at all the evidence in an unbiased way they will see for themselves that it could not possibly be the truth."

PETER JEUCK

Peter was born into the Bible Student movement—the forerunners of Jehovah's Witnesses. His family's involvement with the group stretches all the way back to 1908. With devout parents, including a father bent on moving up the ranks, Peter and his brothers faced a strict upbringing.

"As we approached our teens a good number of us, including me, began rebelling against our parents," he says. "Growing up a Bible Student youth was a crushing experience and anything that took me away from that life seemed like heaven by comparison to that oppressive life."

Peter rebelled so much that he began struggling with alcoholism and getting into fights. "I attended meetings very infrequently and when I did, I'd always be harassed by elders who took it upon themselves to chastise me for turning away from the truth."

After becoming convinced that he was a "black sheep" in need of guidance, Peter delighted his parents by returning to the religion. In time, he met his wife, Stephanie (also a Bible Student), and started a family. Despite tumultuous times in their marriage, Peter and Stephanie forged a strong relationship. When Stephanie began suggesting that the Bible Student movement might be an abusive, controlling group that they would be better off without, Peter listened.

"I began researching the origins of the Bible," Peter relates. "Following years of research I not only concluded that the Bible Students were wrong, but I started to give myself permission to question the existence of the Bible's God."

Looking back on his experience, Peter is today relieved that future generations of his family will be spared the ordeal he endured. "I am so grateful that my grandson, whom we see every weekend, will never be trapped in a religion that demands to control how he will think and live."

MELISSA & DYLAN

Melissa was waiting tables at a restaurant when she first met Dylan. "It was my second day on the job, and I knew the instant he smiled up at me that I was in trouble," she says. "Little did I know just how much trouble I was in for."

Dylan had been raised a Jehovah's Witness, but was disfellowshipped at that time. To begin with, Melissa assumed this was no big deal. "I likened it to a slap on the wrist, and let it go," she recalls. But as their relationship deepened, it became apparent that Dylan had been exiled from a controlling group. And incredibly, he wanted to go back in.

Before long, Melissa and Dylan were married and Dylan was successfully reinstated. But it soon became clear that, despite her best efforts to fit in with her husband's faith, she wouldn't be accepted by either Dylan's parents or the congregation unless she got baptized.

She would overhear sisters in the bathroom gossiping about her during meetings. "No topic was off limits," she says. "I learned that my skirts were inappropriate, my house never clean enough, and that I had apparently 'trapped Dylan.'"

Finally it all got too much, and after one especially distasteful talk celebrating the disfellowshipping arrangement, Melissa decided to quit attending meetings. Dylan followed soon after in a show of solidarity. He tells me that despite occasional anxiety, he is deeply grateful to his wife for gently nudging him toward freedom.

"I am scared somedays," says Dylan. "I think what if my wife had given up on me before I woke up? Where would I be? Would I still be an active JW? Would I have dug in deeper to try to prove her wrong? I truly owe her a debt that cannot be repaid."

NOTES

The following list contains the sources for any quotes in the text that are not already clearly stated. Some Watchtower publications are abbreviated as follows:

- w = Zion's Watch Tower, The Watch Tower or The Watchtower,
- g = The Golden Age, Consolation or Awake!;
- km = Kingdom Ministry, Our Kingdom Ministry or Our Christian Life and Ministry—Meeting Workbook;

Quotes from audio/video sources are numbered in brackets—e.g. "(01)"—to indicate where they can be located in the "Audio and Video Sources" section of my website https://www.reluctantapostate.co

CHAPTER ONE—"LORD, WHOM SHALL WE GO AWAY TO?"

1. "Jehovah's spirit and blessings are linked": w10 9/15 p. 18, par. 7.
2. "By cutting off association with Christ": w08 11/15 p. 14, par. 11.
3. "I feel no need to 'go' anywhere": Crisis of Conscience, p. 406.
4. "Paradoxically, we know more": The Bible For Grown-Ups, p. 9.
5. "We know extraordinarily little": The Bible For Grown-Ups, p. 141.
6. "What if we individually have difficulty": w96 7/15 p. 17, par. 7.

CHAPTER TWO—RESEARCH, RESEARCH, RESEARCH!

1. "The publications and research tools provided": w97 1/15 p. 6.
2. "Our lives depend on spiritual food": km 5/96 p. 1, par. 4.
3. "Of course, there are some topics and scriptures": w11 10/15 p. 32.
4. "Apostates capitalize on errors": w92 7/15 p. 13, par. 19.
5. "Do what God requires of you": w06 11/15 p. 24, par. 17.
6. "Suppose that a doctor told you": w11 7/15 p. 16, par. 6.
7. "He has definitely broken off membership" (ftn.): Organized to Do Jehovah's Will (2015), p. 70.

8. "Keep in mind that Satan": *w17.07* pp. 28-29.

9. "Therefore, it is likely to be most effective": *Media and Society in the Twentieth Century*, p. 83.

10. "As a soldier of Christ" (ftn.): *w60* 6/1 p. 352.

Chapter Three—Planning Your Exit

1. "Persons who make themselves": *w81* 9/15 p. 23, par. 16.

2. "Only God, as he looks at your hands": Anthony Morris talk (01).

3. "Loyal Christians would not associate": "Loyally Uphold Jehovah's Judgments (Symposium)—Shun Unrepentant Wrongdoers" (2016 convention talk outline; ref. *CO-tk16*-E No. 15 11/15)

4. "So, for example, if they had become": Geoffrey Jackson testimony (02).

Chapter Four—Elders Are Not on Your Side

1. "Deliberately spreading teachings contrary": *"Shepherd the Flock of God"—1 Peter 5:2*, pp. 65-66.

2. "Whereas disfellowshipping is an action": *Ibid.*, p. 110.

3. "Making known a firm decision to be known": *Ibid.*, p. 111.

4. "had no more right to this information": *The Reluctant Apostate*, p. 189.

Chapter Eight—Seeking Professional Help

1. "You must take responsibility": *Exiting the JW Cult*, p. 13.

2. "If money is a consideration": *Ibid.*, p. 33.

INDEX

15835940R00083

Printed in Great Britain
by Amazon